Love Never Fails

The Power of Love, Legacy, and Unshakable Faith to
Move You from Fear to Freedom

Rolanda Montenegro

Love Never Fails
The Power of Love, Legacy, and Unshakable Faith to Move You from Fear to Freedom

Copyright © 2025 Rolanda Montenegro

All rights reserved. No portion of this book may be reproduced in any form without permission from the publisher except as permitted by U.S. copyright law. For permissions, contact coachrolanda@gmail.com.

Printed in the United States of America.
First Edition: January 2026

Scripture quotations taken from the Holy Bible, New International Version®, NIV®. Copyright ©1973, 1978, 1984, 2011 by Biblica, Inc.™ Used by permission. All rights reserved worldwide.

Scripture taken from the New King James Version®. Copyright © 1982 by Thomas Nelson. Used by permission. All rights reserved.

Scripture quotations are from King James Version (KJV).

Scripture quotations from THE MESSAGE. Copyright © 1993, 1994, 1995, 1996, 2000, 2001, 2002 by Eugene H. Peterson. Used by permission of NavPress. All rights reserved.

Scripture quotations taken from the Holy Bible, New Living Translation, copyright © 1996, 2004, 2015 by Tyndale House Foundation. Used by permission of Tyndale House Publishers, Carol Stream, Illinois 60188. All rights reserved.

ISBN: 979-8-9935919-0-2

Cover design by Kayla Gavigan
Photo credit by Daniel Groves
Published by Rolanda Montenegro

DEDICATION

To my Dad, whose love, care, and unforgettable hugs showed me what God's love looks like. And to my beautiful Mom, whose strength and perseverance never waver and continue to inspire me. I am forever grateful for both of you.

ACKNOWLEDGMENTS

First and foremost, I give all the glory to God, whose grace and unfailing love made this book possible.

To my husband, Gerard — thank you for your unwavering love and dedication, and for always supporting my dreams. Your love means everything to me. Let's keep going forever!

To my beautiful children, Kayla, Devon, and Gee, you are some of the greatest gifts I've ever received. I'm so honored to be your momma. I am truly grateful for each of you — your love for God and others is a wonderful testimony of grace.

To my two sons-in-love and my daughter-in-love, you all bring great joy, love, and grace to our family! I'm so thankful for each of you!

To my beautiful grandchildren, you are my greatest joy! I love you to pieces and a million made-up songs!

To my mom and sisters, I appreciate your constant support and encouragement.

To my mother-in-love, thank you for being you and for raising an incredible son for me to love.

To all my family and friends who have supported me through every season, I sincerely thank you.

To my editor, Keith Long, thank you for helping me give voice to my memories and experiences with such care.

And to Charlana, thank you for guiding me through the process of publishing my first book—I couldn't have done it without you!

And to you, the reader—thank you for picking up this book. My prayer is that my story inspires you to share yours and reminds you that love never fails.

CONTENTS

Introduction

1. Rooted In Faith — 1
2. Preserved For a Purpose — 11
3. A Life Poured Out — 19
4. A Love Story in Hiding — 29
5. And Then There Were Three — 43
6. Growing in Grace — 55
7. A Stairs House — 67
8. This Is Your Healing — 77
9. The Call — 89
10. Put Me In, Coach — 107
11. The One Decision That Changed Everything — 119
12. Cancer Free — 135
13. Overcoming In Him — 155

INTRODUCTION

"Love never fails." 1 Corinthians 13:8 NKJV

You're stuck. You want more. But something is holding you back—fear, self-doubt, past mistakes, or maybe just the heavy weight of daily life. I've been there too.

I have good news. You don't have to stay there.

I've seen God move through the mess and bring beauty from ashes. Love—His steadfast, unshakable, never-failing love—changed everything for me. It still does. And it can for you too.

Come with me as I pour out my heart. Come with me as I share my life experiences, the stories I've lived, and His unwavering love. Come experience the love only He has to offer—simply for the asking. Because of His love, I am no longer stuck.

I didn't always want to share my story. In fact, for years, I kept parts of my story hidden, tucked away because reliving the moments felt too painful or too private to share. I believe that there's power in our story. There's healing in the telling. And if my story can unlock hope for even one person, then it's worth it.

I'm writing to the woman who feels unseen. To the man who's quietly questioning his worth. To the young person wondering if their life matters. You're not alone. You were made on purpose, for a purpose.

One of my favorite Scriptures says, "Love never fails". (1 Corinthians 13:8) Those three words have carried me through some of my most challenging moments. When life didn't make sense, when prayers felt unanswered, when I didn't feel worthy of love—God reminded me that His love never fails. That's the heartbeat of this book. Not that I have it all figured out, but that I've come to know the One who has it all figured out, who holds it all together—and His love has never let me go. His love never will!

Chapter 1: Rooted in Faith

Let your roots grow down into him, and let your lives be built on him. Then your faith will grow strong in the truth you were taught, and you will overflow with thankfulness.
Colossians 2:7 NLT

Preacher's Kids live under close observation. "PK's." If you know, you know.

My dad was a pastor, so I was a PK. PK's tend to have a reputation, and not always a good one. We live in a fishbowl, under close observation. Many people are unaware of the unique challenges of growing up in a pastor's home. There's this silent pressure to be perfect because your parents are pastors. But nothing could be further from the truth.

On the positive side, I was raised in a Christian home. I was fortunate to be born into a family where God was truly prioritized. Was it a perfect home? Not at all. There were many flaws, but both of my parents loved the Lord wholeheartedly, and they genuinely aimed to follow His perfect will throughout their lives. I am very thankful to be part of that legacy.

It taught me how to fight— for faith, for truth, and to do the right thing even when it's hard.

The reality is, in a pastor's home, a family must walk out their faith with even greater intention. The enemy doesn't let up once you've committed your life to God's work; he fights even harder. If it isn't the enemy throwing darts, it's people. Ministry life isn't easy. But despite all the challenges, I wouldn't trade it for anything. It taught me how to fight for faith, for truth, and to do the right thing even when it's tough.

Some of my favorite childhood memories are family trips to the beach, and I can still see it vividly. I felt like I was on top of the world, sitting on my dad's shoulders in the water. Even more exciting was when he threw me into the waves! Those were the best days. We weren't thinking about the weight of ministry or others' expectations. We got to be just a family, like everyone else.

Maybe that's why I love the beach so much today. It reminds me of those moments — simple, joyful, unhurried. No pressure. No performance. Only love, laughter, and the feeling of being fully present.

Don't get me wrong, ministry is beautiful, and I'm so thankful for the calling on our family's life, but it can also be heavy at times. Ministry costs something. That is why days of rest have become sacred to me. I value them deeply, not just for what they give my body, but for what they give my heart. Those beach days weren't vacations; they were small gifts of peace, joy, and restoration that I now see as vital.

That moment planted something in me that I carried for years: fear.

One life-changing memory from those early years stands out in a very different way. When I was little, I used to sing in church, and I loved it. But one day, while I was singing, I saw people laughing. They thought I was adorable—a little girl with a big voice—but I didn't see it that way at the time. My young heart interpreted their laughter as mockery, and I thought they were making fun of me. That moment planted something in me that I carried for years: fear.

My parents tried to reassure me, telling me again and again,

"They weren't laughing at you, they thought you were cute!" I couldn't believe it. The enemy had already slipped in with a lie, twisting something innocent into something painful. That lie told me I wasn't good enough, that people rejected me, and that I should never get up in front of others again, for fear of what they might say or do next. And I believed that lie.

It was spiritual warfare. Now I know, without a doubt.

For years, I didn't sing. I wouldn't step in front of people. I hid the gift God placed inside me—my voice. It was spiritual warfare. Now I know, without a doubt, the enemy recognized the call of God on my life even before I understood it myself. He knew the power that would come from my voice, in song, speech, and now writing. He tried to shut it down before it ever had the chance to grow.

Are you living in fear? Has the enemy lied to you about your gift? Have the unintentional or intentional actions or words of others caused you to suppress the pursuit of your heart's dreams? God hasn't given up on you. He is still ready to help you become everything He created you to be. He still offers freedom.

Gaining freedom has taken a long time, but I've come to see that moment for what it truly was: an early battle in a much larger war over my identity. Honestly, that's part of why I'm so tender toward children now when they sing or speak in front of others. I never want a child to feel what I felt then: rejected, mocked, or ashamed. That seed of rejection took root in me, and for a long time, it grew into fear, insecurity, and silence.

God is the ultimate Redeemer, and I'm living proof that no lie of the enemy is stronger than the truth of God's love.

Love Never Fails. He's been so faithful in healing those places in me. He's helped me see the truth—that what the enemy meant for harm, God can use for good. That moment didn't define me, but it did shape me. And even now, as I write these words, I see how that lie of rejection tried to follow me through many seasons of my life. God is the ultimate Redeemer, and I'm living proof that no lie of the enemy is stronger than the truth of God's love. If you have a revelation of God's love, you have everything you need. Why? Because His love never fails.

Years later, I started singing again and gradually let go of the fear that had haunted my talent for so long. I have always loved theater and taking on different roles. The chance to become someone else seemed exciting and challenging at the same time. I discovered I was good at it, and throughout elementary, middle, and high school, I participated in choir, ensemble groups, and theater.

Meanwhile, I felt an urge in my heart to follow my big sister's sport of cheerleading. I know some of you might be laughing right now. I understand, but cheerleading can be (and to me, is) a sport because I worked hard at it! I was a flyer, and although I loved being on top, it wasn't fun when I fell to the bottom of a pyramid or stunt.

I learned the value of teamwork and realized I generally preferred having guy friends. I did have a few loyal girlfriends, but I found that sometimes it caused drama in my life. I didn't like drama and always tried to keep the peace.

God knew that it would be woven into my DNA!

From middle school through high school, I was a cheerleader and loved encouraging others and getting the crowd involved in the game. I had no idea how much supporting others would become a part of my future. God knew that it would be woven into my DNA!

Growing up in ministry, most of my friends were part of the church community. As I listened to my dad preach week after week, attending youth services and summer camps, I had many chances to hear the Word and deepen my faith. I loved God, and I knew He loved me too. I never doubted His love, so I am genuinely thankful to have received that revelation at such a young age. I have continued to grow in this revelation, and I know I have only just begun to understand it.

My parents helped me realize that God loved me unconditionally.

My parents helped me realize that God loved me unconditionally. As you will see, that would be very important as my life progressed. I was significantly impacted by them showing God's unconditional love and care for others. My dad was a preacher. My mom ministered to many women over the years, encouraging them to prioritize God's Word and obey it. She was and still is a passionate prayer warrior. Many say more is caught than taught, and I believe that is often true.

I recall that in high school, some of my friends would host parties, and although they liked me, I was never invited. That didn't offend me at all because I had no desire to hang out in that environment. It wasn't my thing. I was confident in my skin and never really tried to fit in. I know that was a result of being rooted in faith, my family's love, and God's love for me. I so recognize and appreciate my parents' love for God and their desire to train my sisters and me in His word.

His Perfect Plan

I don't know your story, or your parents, or how your

upbringing influenced where you are today. But I do know it's never too late to place your trust in Him. He can change your heart, bringing you to a place where you can overflow with gratitude, knowing each step of your journey, good or bad, can be used for your good in His perfect plan.

A bit about my dad before we take the next step in this journey. His life and upbringing greatly shaped my life and my testimony.

When I began to share my story, I never expected I would also share his. In truth, this originally started as his book. Sadly, he only wrote a few pages before COVID ended his life. However, God spoke to my heart, telling me that people need to hear it.

Love Never Fails would not mean much without the love my dad showed me on both his good and bad days. As you will see, our relationship wasn't perfect. But the seeds of love planted throughout my life let my roots grow deep in faith. Now I overflow with thankfulness that our relationship was restored into a beautiful masterpiece of what happens when Love Never Fails.

Chapter 2: Preserved for a Purpose

Preserve me, O God, for in You I put my trust.
Psalm 16:1 NKJV

Dad was raised by a woman who was legally blind. Born near the end of the Great Depression in 1937, he was the third of five children. Under these adverse circumstances, he would learn about family, hard work, and faith.

"Granny" was one of the strongest women I've ever known. I am still amazed at how she managed. Despite her vision limitations, she had the most beautiful flower garden I have ever seen. The rich variety of scents was only matched by the array of vibrant colors. She couldn't see the blooms with her own eyes, but her other senses were much sharper than mine. She also made the best homemade biscuits and black-eyed peas I have ever tasted.

Daddy and Granny (his mother)

Dad grew up very poor. He often talked about his early life in the projects. Most of the clothes he wore were hand-me-downs that were way too big. Other kids would make fun of him, and that ridicule motivated him to get his first job as soon as he was old enough—picking cotton in the fields. A truck would come by early in the morning to pick them up from the slums and take him and the others out into the cotton fields to work a full day. He worked hard to earn enough money to buy clothes that fit. That put an end to the teasing for good.

Roots of Dad's Faith

Their home wasn't just a house; it was the place where their church first started. I love that story. I am so blessed to have such a spiritual legacy. Even as a young boy, my dad was surrounded by faith beyond his ability to understand how much it affected him.

The burdens of poverty fostered one of the biggest strongholds—fear.

Everyone in the family loved Jesus and knew about God. But even in a faith-filled home, there were strongholds. The burdens of poverty fostered one of the biggest strongholds—fear. My grandfather, my dad's father, was a talented man. I grew up with my father's stories of his father selling boiled peanuts by the roadside. He didn't earn much doing it, but one day someone offered him a much better-paying job. Out of fear that he'd fail, he turned it down. That story has always stayed with me. Fear had such a firm hold on him that he couldn't even try. And that fear didn't stop with him, it became generational. It affected my dad, and honestly, it affected me too.

It has taken me years to start writing this book, and fear is the reason. Fear of rejection. Fear of failure. Fear that it won't be good enough. That no one will read it. But I'm doing it anyway because I know it matters. And I know it's time to tell my story. Love never fails.

Someone needs your story.

Perhaps you also have a story to share, and fear has held you back. My prayer is that this will spark something in you—to stop letting fear hold your message captive. I pray you'll courageously share what God has done in your life with anyone willing to listen. Someone needs your story. With His help and love, you too can break free from fear and become all He created you to be.

As a child, my dad knew about God but wasn't fully committed to following Him. Before he passed, he began writing about his life before Christ and the spiritual battles he had experienced. He firmly believed that the enemy had tried to take him out multiple times before he ever gave his heart to Jesus. One of those times, he was a little boy standing too close to the fireplace when he caught on fire. Thankfully, his father was nearby and put out the flames.

Around age 10, he tried to follow his sisters to the ice cream parlor. They didn't want him tagging along, so he sneaked behind them. As he crossed the street, he was hit by a car and knocked out. He regained consciousness and, after visiting the doctor, was miraculously okay.

The third time was when he was about 13. His dad gave him a Western Flyer bicycle for Christmas. He loved that bike. He and his friends enjoyed taking apart bicycles and rebuilding them to see how they worked. One day, while working on bikes, a curious friend poured gasoline into a cup of hot grease to see what would happen.

He threw in a match, and the can exploded into flames! My dad instinctively grabbed the flaming can and tossed it away to protect them, but the fire spilled down the side of his head, burning him badly. He remembered pacing the floor in searing pain. His father looked at him and said, "Son, you'd better remember this and get right with God. Hell is very hot, and you don't want to go there."

Although surrounded by believers, my dad wondered why no one had ever tried to lead him in a prayer of salvation. He attended church, youth rallies, and revivals, but he usually left right after the preaching, slipping out with his friends before the altar call. Still, everyone was praying for him, trusting that God's power would touch his life.

"Lord, if you let me get to church tonight, I'll give my life to you."

Everything changed when he was 18. He had just finished high school and was planning to meet a girl, but she had another guy there too. Frustrated, he jumped into his car and sped off, weaving through traffic. Suddenly, he saw a car coming out of the valley heading straight toward him. He hit the brakes and lost control—his vehicle slid off the road, spun around, but didn't flip over. In that terrifying moment, he cried out to God, "Lord, if you let me get to church tonight, I'll give my life to you."

He made it to church that night. On the way, a police officer pulled him over. The officer didn't give him a ticket but said, "Son, it's bad enough to kill yourself, but worse to take others with you." That warning hit him hard. God had spared him again.

Love Came In

That night at church, he sat at the back with his friend Ethan. When the evangelist closed his Bible, Ethan leaned over and said, "Let's go." Ethan thought they were heading outside as they usually did after the sermon, but my dad said, "No. We're going to the altar." That night, he gave his life to Jesus. Everything changed. Love came in.

At first, he doubted himself. He didn't fully grasp what had happened in his heart. He wondered if he was truly saved—until his Sunday school teacher at church told him, "If you asked Jesus into your heart, then you are forgiven." That moment stayed with him. He said it was like a light turning on deep inside. He exclaimed, "Well, I'm saved then!" and everyone rejoiced. That was the moment his spirit caught up with his faith—and he never looked back.

I love how he described it—so simple, yet so powerful.

I love how he described it—so simple, yet so powerful. It reminds me of Romans 10:9-10, "If you declare with your mouth, 'Jesus is Lord,' and believe in your heart that God raised him from the dead, you will be saved." He led hundreds, if not thousands, of people in that simple prayer after his conversion.

Four times, Satan tried to take him out. And four times, God protected him for a purpose. There are even more stories he didn't write about, but these are the ones he documented. Now, I am honored to help finish telling them for him.

If love hasn't found you yet, please remember, He is waiting for you. He is prepared to give you more than you could ever imagine. He is ready to come into your heart, forgive your sins, and welcome you into His family—for eternity. As dad would say, "It's so simple, yet so powerful."

When I began this journey, I didn't know it would be a tribute to my dad. But that's precisely what it has become. He didn't get to finish his book, but I'm putting it on paper now. For my healing. For your benefit. For His glory.

I believe in my heart that would make him smile.

Chapter 3: A Life Poured Out

But I will rejoice even if I lose my life, pouring it out like a liquid offering to God, just like your faithful service is an offering to God. And I want all of you to share that joy.
Philippians 2:17 NLT

"After Dairold saw Bettye up there on the organ with that mini sweater on, he was no good to me." The words of an evangelist rang true, and life would never be the same.

Finding Jesus changed my dad's life more than he expected. Everything in his life started to align with God's purpose, and God was shaping him for his true calling.

He worked in construction and bookkeeping while learning to manage departments effectively. His natural leadership skills quickly became clear and were fully evident. These abilities grew stronger because of his integrity, loyalty, faithfulness, and especially his genuine compassion and care for others.

While in his twenties, he joined a group that traveled to minister to other churches. Like his parents, he loved music—it was in his blood. During a particular ministry trip to Copeland, Alabama, everything changed: he met Bettye.

She had an eighteen-inch waist, high heels, beautiful black hair, and brown eyes. Above all, she loved the Lord with all her heart. We don't call them "mini-sweaters" anymore, but Bettye was a looker even before adding the "mini-sweater." Dad was singing with the minister and his family when he spotted Bettye playing the organ. As the evangelist would later recall, after that "he was no good to me."

I love that so much.

There was one problem: she was dating someone else at the time, a guy who was away at college. That didn't stop my dad. The very next day, he took her for a ride and told her, "You're just the kind of girl I want to be my wife." They had a good time, so my bold, confident dad turned to my mom at one point and said, "I want a kiss, and I don't want any back talk." She leaned in and kissed him, and the rest is history!

If you knew my dad, you'd see how funny he was, especially when telling stories. He made you feel like you were right there with him. Meeting my mom and going on that drive is one of the best stories, and it always made my sisters and me smile. It's one of our family's favorites.

What a love story. What a legacy.

From that moment on, their story began. They married in August 1961 and enjoyed 60 years together before my dad went home to be with the Lord. What a love story. What a legacy.

God Had a Plan for His Life

The day after their wedding, he was ordered to active duty. He had about six weeks before he needed to report, right before the Berlin Crisis. He served for a year and, thanks to his VA benefits, later attended college and earned his bachelor's degree in ministry. He recalls a story about heading to college right after high school with a friend, and something told him not to go. He turned around and went home. Even though he didn't fully understand it at the time, he saw it as divine providence—God had a plan for his life.

August 25, 1961 — the day my parents got married.

Before his time in the service and his full-time ministry, he worked hard at various everyday jobs. He worked at a grocery store doing everything except cutting the meat. He held several management roles and was a schoolteacher, but he always loved painting. Painting brought him joy, not just because it was creative, but because he could step back, see the transformation, and smile, saying, "It always looked better with a paint job." He was a messy painter, like me, but he was the best!

Dad and Mom served together in every part of the church. They led the youth, cared for older adults, and helped wherever needed. He often reflected that, as a young man, he probably spent too much time working and not enough helping my mom with my two older sisters. But he always did his best.

My parents always sang together. A dynamic duo and part of the worship team, they were both musically talented. My mom could play any song by ear in any key on the piano and organ. Her voice was as lovely as a bird singing a joyful tune. Dad's primary instrument was always his voice—strong, clear, passionate—whether singing or preaching to thousands.

Powerfully and beautifully, they sang with perfect pitch.

If you have ever heard them sing together, you would never forget it. Their harmonies were always precise. Powerfully and beautifully, they sang with perfect pitch. Their timing was flawless in every note. Some of my favorites were "Feeling Mighty Fine," "Until Then," and "Goodbye World, Goodbye."

The Call to Ministry

Dad felt called to ministry about five years into their marriage. However, he insisted on getting an education first. He firmly believed in being well-prepared. In about two weeks, they sold their house and moved to Lakeland, Florida, in 1966.

While Dad was in school full-time and working in the men's department at Sears as a salesman, he and Mom continued to serve faithfully. In 1968, before he finished his degree, he was asked to become a senior pastor. He accepted and later earned his bachelor's degree in ministry from Southeastern Bible College. He was deeply thankful to God for that chapter of his life because it gave him a solid foundation for the decades of ministry that followed.

That was my dad: faithful, hardworking, intentional, and highly motivated. Whether he was preaching, singing, building, or painting, he poured his whole heart into it. He showed how to live out his calling with excellence in everything he did.

I love and miss my dad. I'm sharing about him because you,

too, can follow Jesus in pursuing His calling for you. You can start right where you are and accomplish everything you were made to do. God will never give up on you.

Overcoming Fear

He grew deeper in his faith as the years went by and became more involved in the Assemblies of God denomination. As a respected leader, he participated in interviewing new applicants for the ministry. He served as an assistant presbyter, and the leadership team wanted him to step into the full presbyter role. When asked, he initially declined. I asked him why, and he said, "I was fearful, like my daddy." That admission hit me hard. The fear that had held his father seemed to hold him back as well.

Eventually, he trusted God, overcame his fear, stepped into that role—and thrived. He helped many pastors over the years through conflict, crisis, and burnout. He counseled, supported, and encouraged ministers from across the state. His leadership was characterized by compassion, wisdom, and humility. Instead of letting fear hold him back from answering the higher call to reach more people, he embraced God's love to help him overcome.

In his fifty years of pastoral ministry, he built two churches from the ground up—one that seated a thousand people. His construction experience gave him an edge in building projects. At the time, he probably didn't realize why he was working all those different jobs. God was using every season of his life to prepare him for what was ahead. I love how God can use every season we go through, even when it doesn't always make sense.

Sometimes, we do things in life without realizing how they will fit into the bigger picture. But when God is in it, nothing is wasted. He has a way of weaving it all together for our good, just as Scripture tells us in Romans 8:28 (KJV): *"And we know that all things work together for good to them that love God, to them who are the called according to his purpose."* That's what God did for my dad. That's what God did for me.

That's what God is doing for you!

His life revealed the true secret to living in God's will. He achieved success in every building project, leadership opportunity, and ministry role, not because he chased success but because he pursued faithfulness. He dedicated his life to the Gospel. When my dad died in 2021, Nancy Kennedy wrote a beautiful article in the local Citrus County Chronicle. She interviewed my mom, sisters, and me. (chronicleonline.com)

Mercy on a whole new level.

My sister Rhonda shares a story about a man who had a

conflict with my dad and decided to picket outside my dad's church on the church's property. She remembers my dad bringing him food and water while he picketed. It lasted for several days before ending. Later, that man returned to the church, this time to repent. My dad and mom were there for him when he passed away. Mercy on a whole new level.

Many would have written off this man and wanted nothing more than to silence him. Hearing this story, I felt like giving him a piece of my mind. But I know that's not what Daddy would've done. Love never fails.

Like Mom, Daddy was also a prayer warrior. He kept an active, current prayer list, and he didn't pray only for his friends; his enemies were on it too. Although I don't think he ever truly had enemies, at least not in his mind. If he said he would pray for you, he meant it. My mom recalls, "He often said God brought him to Citrus County to help hurting people, and he succeeded." He was a sincere man of God who loved deeply and cared for others like no one else I have ever known. And now, his legacy lives on through my sisters and me and all those who knew him.

I was always a daddy's girl, and I'm sure you can understand why. He was the kind of dad who loved up close; he didn't pass by without giving you a big hug. It made you feel seen and cared for. I'm so thankful for his life.

Chapter 4: A Love Story in Hiding

There is no fear in love; but perfect love casts out fear, because fear involves torment. But he who fears has not been made perfect in love.
1 John 4:18 NKJV

My boyfriend was away at college.

Sometimes, legacy runs deeper than we realize. Sometimes, Jesus frees you from what seems right but isn't truly right for you. I thought I was doing well. I had many friends, was a cheerleader, and had a steady boyfriend away at college. God had a better plan. Like the story of my mom and dad, this was a kind of legacy that was truly good.

It was my junior year in high school. One of my close friends worked at a T-shirt shop when a short, Cuban-descended man walked in, looking to buy shirts for his new business. He was opening a video store called Video City. Impressed with how she managed the company at such a young age, he asked if she wanted to work for him. When she said she would consider the job, he asked if she had any friends. "Yes, I do, but my friend is churchy, churchy, churchy. She is always at church every time the doors are open." His easy laugh assured her he didn't mind at all. Of course, I was that friend.

I got the job and was excited to work at a video store. I had always loved movies and lived near a different store. Before I had my license, I would walk there to pick up a few movies and grab a pizza at Pizza Factory next door. Good memories! This was before DVDs and Redbox, while Blockbuster was still around.

We had not met yet, but I was now intrigued.

My friend and I were at school eating lunch in the cafeteria when a tall, dark, and handsome guy walked by our table. "That's him," she told me. He laughed as he waved to us. His laugh and cute smile got my immediate attention. We had not met yet, but I was now intrigued.

I took a job at Video City, and you can probably guess who

trained me! Yes—the same tall, dark, and handsome boy from the cafeteria. Gerard. From the beginning, we had a great connection; we both loved music and football. On top of his appearance, I loved his laugh. He was the manager of the video store, my boss. He'll tell you the position was only temporary; his father was the owner.

A quick friendship would eventually grow into something more. Like my mom, I broke up with my boyfriend, who was away at college. I trusted God, even though I wasn't entirely sure what He was doing. He was from New York and grew up in a completely different environment than I did. In my mind, he was more street-smart; I was more book-smart. However, I would learn that he's brilliant in every way.

Perfect Love Casts Out Fear, Even for the Imperfect

I have some good news and some bad news for you. The good news is that if you lean into His love, you can overcome any fear. The bad news is that it might still cost you. But I can assure you, His love is worth it. Every single time.

We thought we might be the perfect couple, except for the one thing that set us apart. Not in our eyes, but in the eyes of many others, the color of our skin didn't match. I was white, he was black. In a small town in the South in the late 80s, it wasn't as accepted as it is today. I sadly knew it would not go over very well at home either. But we were determined to see where God was taking us, so we started a relationship. A secret relationship.

... and most of all, he was my friend.

Oh, I wanted to shout it from the rooftops because Gerard was different. He was everything I needed in my life. He was fun, made me laugh, and helped me relax more. I could be myself without feeling judged or pressured to be perfect, and most of all, he was my friend.

From the start, I told him that if he wanted to be with me, he had to come to church. He'll tell you that it was a no-brainer for him, ha-ha! It was good for him too, so he started coming to church with me. I didn't even know he was listening, but I was happy he was there. One night, he asked Jesus to come into his heart. He was saved at my Daddy's church. He never walked up to the altar, but he repeated that prayer right from his seat in the back, right beside me.

Soon after I met Gerard, it was time for a beauty pageant. I had competed the previous two years, placing second runner-up both times. After that year, my age would prevent me from competing again, so I was determined to finally win the crown. I worked hard on my rendition of "New York, New York" by Frank Sinatra, complete with the cutest tuxedo, top hat, and tails for my costume. I felt both excited and nervous! I was confident on stage, but I never felt comfortable during the competition's interview phase. I was afraid of messing up, not making sense, or even not being able to answer their questions. After all, we had no idea what they would ask us, and even though we practiced, it felt like a blank slate when we walked into that room. I was so nervous about forgetting everything, with all eyes on me. The legacy of fear that haunted my grandfather and my dad would follow me into that room.

Then Everything Changed

I won the talent competition, but I didn't do as well in my interview. I had let my fears affect the competition. I finished third runner-up this time, and I was crushed. I now realize it was foolish to be so upset. I can't explain why it affected me so profoundly, but it did.

The very next day, I reached out to my pageant coach, who shared some of the judges' comments. One judge mentioned I had too much cellulite on my thighs. They also shared the mostly positive interview results, but there was one question I didn't handle well. The rejection was more than I could handle. I hung up from that call and told Gerard about the judge's comments. That was the day I lost my virginity. Everything changed after that.

A flood of emotions and guilt washed over my soul like a river. I didn't know what to do. I was so ashamed of what I had done. I was sixteen years old and a junior in high school. I was proud of myself for not giving in for years when most of my friends had. Now, I felt impure, dirty. What was I going to do? I kept this secret hidden, like a mother protecting her little cub, until I couldn't anymore. But that didn't stop me.

When you're down, the enemy hits you the hardest. When you're disappointed, he attacks both your pride and your shame. In those moments, your only defense is to seek God above all else. But even when you don't, there is grace. There is ALWAYS grace. He will be there waiting when you turn to Him, whenever that is, and He will welcome you into the warm embrace of His love. I had to learn it the hard way.

They were firm that I couldn't date him because he was a different race.

A few months later, I went to summer youth camp. I prayed and asked God to forgive me again because we were still very close. I talked to one of the speakers, and he reassured me that it was okay that Gerard was Black and encouraged me to be honest with my parents. Well, I wasn't fully ready for that, so I only hinted that I liked him. They were firm that I couldn't date him because he was of a different race. The secret relationship continued. Intimacy persisted. They could not know.

Both of my parents grew up in Alabama, a deep southern state. Romantic relationships between different races were not acceptable in their era. I didn't understand it because I always had friends of different races or ethnic backgrounds, even though I never dated someone from a different background. Dating would have been a little too close to home.

We kept dating secretly, and in January of 1990, during our senior year of high school, I became pregnant. I was unsure of what to do. I called my sister first, and she helped me find peace. She said she would tell them for me, and I agreed that would be best.

But God's love was about to come through.

They were devastated and didn't know how to handle it. It wasn't what they expected for my future. They wanted me to graduate from high school and follow my dad's footsteps by going to college in Lakeland. It wasn't part of the plan. It wasn't part of my plan either, but then it became that way.

I remember debating abortion in high school. The conversations would get very heated, even among friends. People supported a woman's right to choose, especially in cases of rape.

However, in my heart, I could never see that as the right choice. I fought for life. I often wondered whether some of them had asked what I would do now that I was pregnant.

    My parents and I started counseling immediately. The counselor gave us helpful advice: to let Gerard and me talk, see each other, and figure out what we wanted to do, and what God wanted us to do. It was okay for a day or two, but then we weren't allowed to talk or see each other again. I was so stressed it made me sick. I kept going to school, cheering, and working. I attended church and youth events. Life looked normal from the outside, but it was not. No one knew except us. I was living in a nightmare with no light at the end of the tunnel. But God's love was about to come through. And come through in a big way.

    An appointment was scheduled for all of us to see the counselor—Gerard, his parents, my parents, and me. The counselor thought we all needed to meet to help us connect and get through this tough time. But something inside didn't sit right with me. I told my parents I wouldn't be going, and they didn't like that, showing their frustration. I didn't see the point in talking when we weren't even following the advice we had already been given. I'd never seen my parents like that before, and I felt unsure of what to do. My dad was so upset. As they left the room, arguing, I made a life-changing decision.

I can feel what I felt—scared, rejected, unsure of my present and future, and so ashamed.

I called Gerard and asked him to meet me at the end of the street. As soon as I hung up the phone, I packed my bags, grabbed some saltine crackers, and ran out the back door. As I ran, I held my stomach and prayed to God to help me and protect my baby. I will never forget that run. I can still see it now when I close my eyes. I can feel what I felt—scared, rejected, unsure of my present and future, and so ashamed. But still, in that moment, because of the faith and love that had been planted deep down in my heart, I knew I could call on the mighty name of Jesus. That's exactly what I did.

Gerard picked me up and we went to my sister's house. I knew I couldn't stay there, so their pastor took me in. They lived in a gated community and could shield me from the conflict that had surrounded me for the past few weeks. Their goal was for me to pray, rest, and listen for God's guidance on what He wanted us to do. While I was there, they allowed Gerard to call me, and they even gave us the chance to go on a real date, which we had never really done because our relationship had always been kept a secret.

Life can be messy and painful at times, but we must keep moving forward.

Keeping secrets leads to a life full of lies. I lived one lie after another, and it was eating away at me from the inside. I'm not proud of what I did or how I was living. I can't change the past, but I won't only share the good parts of my life. It is my prayer that others can find freedom in Jesus as I share my story. I pray you can find freedom in Jesus and let go of shame.

Life can be messy and painful at times, but we must keep moving forward. Before getting pregnant, I can remember going to the altar every Sunday night to repent and ask God for forgiveness for having sex before marriage. I knew it was wrong, but I was trapped in my choices.

I spent a few days with my sisters' pastors, then I talked with my parents. Nothing had changed. They still didn't want us to see each other or plan a future together. I was really discouraged and stressed out. At that point, we decided to elope. In Florida at that time, if you were a 17-year-old girl and pregnant, you didn't need your parents' permission to get married. Gerard was still 17 and needed his parents' permission, and they consented.

The day before we got married, the couple I was staying with took me shopping and bought me a beautiful white suit to wear. Although I didn't feel very pure, she gave me a small glimmer of hope that everything would be okay. She encouraged me and created a safe space for me to think and process, which I am forever grateful for.

The Hands and Feet of Jesus

You never know how God can use you in life to help someone else during a crisis, but I believe it's an opportunity to be God's hands and feet for others. She helped me, and I hope these words of confession and encouragement inspire you. God is faithful and will see you through the toughest times.

In ministry life, we often encounter moments when we need to be the hands and feet of Jesus. My parents frequently faced these times with the people they ministered to at their church and in their community. I was so confused about why I wasn't receiving the same love and acceptance they showed others. However, this time was different. I know it wasn't intentional, but the feeling of rejection I experienced was deep, like nothing I had ever felt before. The burden was heavy, but God's love was always present, and He carried me through every step.

I'm not upset with my parents about what happened. How could I be? In fact, they are the two people who introduced me to His unconditional love, and without them, I wouldn't know that kind of love. I think we expect the people in our lives to always be perfect and to accept us unconditionally. Whether that's true or not, it's not always realistic or possible. Nobody is perfect. People are just people. They hurt, and often hurt others in turn. It's true when they say, "hurt people, hurt people." Now that my children are all adults, I realize I've made plenty of mistakes I wish I could take back. Of course, we can't, but we learn from each one.

On January 31, 1990, we drove to the courthouse, where a slightly older woman with a raspy throat and a tube in her neck performed our ceremony. I'll never forget her. We said, "I do," and we've been saying it ever since. After the ceremony, we went to his parents' house, where they had a lovely cake, and his family gathered to celebrate our new union.

We decided to take a couple of days off to visit Disney World and enjoy a brief honeymoon before returning to school and work. I took a deep breath and called my parents. I told them I was married and hung up.

January 31, 1990 - the day Gerard and I became one. We were 17 years old and seniors in high school.

Chapter 5: And Then There Were Three

He knows us far better than we know ourselves, knows our pregnant condition, and keeps us present before God. That's why we can be so sure that every detail in our lives of love for God is worked into something good.
Romans 8:27-28 MSG

"There's something to be said about spending time with the Timeless One." Words of wisdom from my Florida pastor. Every moment with Jesus gives you confidence when you need it most. He provides the wisdom, the answers, and the resources you are believing for. He is always faithful—even when we are not!

We were married and needed Jesus more than ever. We were almost done with high school and determined to walk the stage together with our class. Once we returned from our short, sweet honeymoon, I went to the principal's office to ask for his help. I'll never forget his kindness and his lack of judgment.

I needed to finish two classes to graduate. I told him I didn't want to go back to school, but I still wanted to graduate with my class. How does that even work? His grace was there every step of the way. The principal told me that if I enrolled in a prenatal course at the local vocational school and completed the remaining two classes there, he would let me walk the stage with my friends.

Love never fails.

We had moved to that small town when I was in second grade. I built a life there, with friendships that meant a great deal to me, and I wanted nothing more than to share that moment with them. And just like that, God made a way. I still don't know where the courage came from to walk into that office with such a bold request, but I know God was with me. Love never fails.

Here we were, seventeen years old, kids having a kid, balancing work and school. Everything in my life shifted in just a few short weeks. The shock was real, and honestly, I don't know how we got through it. That's not entirely true, I DO know how we got through it. God made a way, and we let Him. I know we wouldn't have made it without Him.

We stayed with Gerard's parents for the first couple of weeks. I wish I could remember more of that time, but everything's fuzzy. Maybe it was all the stress before that season, or the stress that lingered after. But I can tell you, post-traumatic stress is real.

We had nothing. No money, no furniture, no plan, except to be together and build a life.

His parents helped us find a place to live. And when I say helped, I truly mean they did. We had nothing—no money, no furniture, no plan—except to be together and build a life. And that's exactly what we did.

We found a charming two-bedroom, one-bathroom apartment not far from my parents' house, and it became our first home. His parents helped us furnish it, and we received a thoughtful shower to help us with the essentials. My parents also came over to help, and gradually, we started to repair what had been broken. We never discussed it openly, but somehow, I had a sense that things would be okay.

We graduated from high school in June 1990. By then, I was six months pregnant, and it was noticeable. I walked across the stage and received my diploma right behind my husband, with my new name,

Rolanda Rushing Montenegro. I could sense some criticism, but I didn't let it bother me. I was so thankful to finish, even though it was one of the toughest seasons of my life.

Our High School Graduation, June 1990

God walked across that stage with both of us. He's ready to walk with you, too, across whatever stage you must cross. Post-traumatic stress is real, but God's love is infinitely more real.

A Girl Dad—and Granddad

Our baby's arrival was near, and my mom hosted a baby shower for me at the church. That was such a blessing. God began to heal our relationship. He was working. He was restoring. I still have an old video of me showing my dad the baby's room, complete with the adorable frilly dresses, Mickey and Minnie Mouse bedding, baby furniture, and toys.

I was so proud to show him that room. He was excited to welcome a new grandbaby. I've always been a daddy's girl; we just always clicked. He was a "girl dad," with three daughters and no sons. When I was born, he thought for sure he was finally going to get a boy. He even painted the nursery blue in anticipation. Surprise! I was not a boy. But he was okay with that. I came out with a head full of dark hair and big brown eyes, and he was in love.

Dad was in his mid-thirties when I was born, a bit older than he was when my sisters arrived. That might have given him more wisdom or patience. I don't know. But no parent, regardless of their age, does everything perfectly.

He always attended my games. While I cheered for the team, he cheered for me. He encouraged me in my singing and always believed in my voice. He pushed me to speak in public even when I lacked confidence. He would even read the Word to me while I did my makeup in the mornings before school, sitting on the edge of the tub. The "seat" was uncomfortable, but he didn't care. He knew how important it was for me to start my day with the Word of God.

It taught me to forgive and to watch God take a shattered situation and piece it back together.

Yes, when I got pregnant, the disappointment was real. I knew I had hurt him deeply. He didn't respond the way I hoped, but I never doubted that he loved me. He was hurting too. So was my mom. And they did the best they could. It hurt. Deeply. But it also made me grow. It taught me to forgive and to watch God take a shattered situation and piece it back together.

I've read stories of others supported from day one when they got pregnant. And sure, I've compared. I've wondered why that wasn't my story. But my parents were both full of God and fully human. The disappointment may have been louder than the grace I needed. I don't know. And honestly? I don't need to know. Because the redemption of my story is worth every ounce of despair I felt.

We often ask, "Why me?" but maybe that's not the right question. Perhaps we're meant to respond with honor, praise, and trust. We might worship through the chaos. What felt like my world falling apart was a beautiful God story being written right before my eyes.

Words Can Bring Life or Death

Sometimes we speak out of our pain, saying things we don't truly mean. Our words can bring life or death (Proverbs 18:21). But God can take the darkest parts of your story and turn them into a magnificent masterpiece. And that's precisely what He did.

Our beautiful baby girl was born on August 29, 1990. She arrived five days early, and I was perfectly fine with that! Babies have a way of changing the atmosphere, and that's precisely what she did.

At seventeen, I received a title I would cherish forever, "Mom." Becoming a mother changed everything for me. The moment I held her in my arms, I felt a love I had never experienced before. I was overwhelmed in the best way. Her tiny fingers, how she fit perfectly on my chest, the little coos she made — it felt like time stopped. Despite all the chaos and uncertainty of our situation, she brought us unbelievable joy.

All the fear, shame, and confusion took a backseat to the deep love I had for this baby girl.

When the nurse asked if I wanted to hold her, that first time, I still remember thinking, "Wow, we made this little person." What a miracle. I was young, unsure of what the future held, yet I knew I would do anything to protect her. My heart now lived outside my body. All the fear, shame, and confusion took a backseat to the deep love I had for this baby girl.

Of course, I had no idea what I was doing. I was still a teenager, still trying to figure out who I was, and now I was responsible for another life. But even when I felt unsure, God assured me that I wasn't alone. He had entrusted me with this precious gift, and He would guide me every step of the way. He has never stopped doing that!

My parents were so happy to meet her and especially to hold her in their arms. I remember my dad talking to her in the hospital room. We brought her home, and my mom was there to help me and love on her new little granddaughter. She bathed her, changed her diaper, rocked her to sleep, and, while I struggled with nursing, kept encouraging me to keep trying, and I did. Fortunately, we figured it out, and I'm so glad. I know not everyone can, but breastfeeding was such a sweet time with all three of my babies.

God Changes the Odds

Two became three, and we couldn't imagine life without her. This tiny human has become part of our lives, and she has changed us for the better. We realized how important it is to work hard despite the odds. Research shows that only a small percentage of teen parents end up marrying each other, and teen marriages have some of the highest risks of breaking apart. Teen relationships face pressures they aren't emotionally or financially prepared for. By every measure, we shouldn't have lasted. Yet grace held us together. To everyone's surprise, my husband and I, being an interracial couple, are still married today!

Before her, I mostly worried about fitting in and whether people liked me—things a typical teenager would stress over. After all, I was one. But once she arrived, none of that seemed to matter anymore. My focus shifted. I wanted to be better for her. Not perfect, by any means, but there. I might not have had a big plan, but I had a big reason. God had the big plan.

God has a big plan for you, too.

I was so blessed that motherhood came naturally to me. Even though I was young, I was never really into the party scene in high school, so I never felt like I missed out on being young and free. Most of my friends were heading to college, but I was starting my journey into parenthood. I never once felt like my life was going in a direction I didn't love. I was so happy to be with my new husband and our new baby. Even though we were young and broke, we had each other and our little one, and that meant everything.

After our baby girl was a few months old, we moved into his parents' rental property a few miles away. We had more space, which was nice as our baby girl was starting to get around more. After she turned one year old, we moved again, this time to another city so that Gerard could pursue one of his dreams. He always loved music and wanted to be a recording engineer someday. So, we relocated to Orlando, and he attended a recording engineering school.

God provided. He made a way in the desert.

I started working full-time, while our daughter was in daycare, as Gerard worked part-time and attended school full-time. We found a good church and started serving immediately. We had the smallest apartment you could imagine, and our daughter's crib happened to fit perfectly inside the extra closet, so that became her new room. It wasn't ideal, but it was our tiny home. Both of our parents supported us during those times, especially my dad. We faced serious financial struggles, and I realize much of it was because we didn't know how to budget our money and weren't faithful in giving.

I knew what the Bible said about tithing, and I believed in it. However, it seemed like we were so broke, and Gerard wasn't quite convinced how we could give 10% of our income and still live on the 90% when even 100% of our revenue wasn't enough. In Malachi chapter 3, it talks about bringing all your tithes and offerings into the storehouse, which means your church home, and God says to "Test me in this…see if I won't open the windows of heaven and pour out a blessing you can't even contain."

This teaching was new to Gerard, but I told him we would keep struggling unless we started putting God first. So, we began tithing, and I can't remember a time when we didn't have what we needed each month. God provided. He made a way in the desert. That's simply who He is and what He does. He is so faithful; He never changes.

He will always be faithful to you, too. Trust Him.

Chapter 6: Growing in Grace

*Rather, you must grow in the grace and knowledge
of our Lord and Savior Jesus Christ.
All glory to him, both now and forever! Amen.*
2 Peter 3:18 NLT

We didn't realize it back then, but that church in Ocala would become our home—a place of healing, growth, and grace. From the moment we stepped inside, it felt different. The worship was incredible. The Word was alive. The people were genuine. We found the community we didn't even know we needed. We looked at each other and both knew we were home, so we made it ours, and it became one of the best decisions we've ever made.

It was early 1994. We had two beautiful girls and another baby on the way. Life had already knocked us around quite a bit. We were only 21 and still trying to figure things out. We learned the hard way that even if the bank sends you a box of checks, only one person should carry the checkbook. We initially bounced several checks because we failed to communicate about our spending habits. You could call this part of growing up. We were young and dumb.

Finding this new church home was a season when we truly began to grow—not just in our relationships, but most importantly in our faith. We learned how to live by it and how to get along with each other. Our hearts were open, and our minds were being renewed. For the first time I can remember, we discovered how powerful our words are and how much our thinking influences our lives.

I lacked a genuine revelation of what Jesus had already done for me.

Although I was raised in church and knew God as a PK, I still had a lot of unlearning to do. Somehow, I clung to law-based thinking and beliefs instead of grace. I learned a lot about 'don't do this and don't do that,' but I lacked a genuine revelation of what

Jesus had already done for me. I'm sure I heard these powerful truths before, but I hadn't truly understood them. When you hear something, it doesn't cause a drastic change in your life until it becomes real to you.

Grace is Jesus Personified

I began learning about God's righteousness and how, when I believed in Him, I was considered righteous—not because of my works or performance, but simply because I believed. This revelation was a turning point for me. Our pastor spoke about God's grace, and it was like music to my ears. God was clarifying all the misunderstandings I had and replacing them with truth. We were learning that grace wasn't just a concept—it was a way of life, and it was Jesus personified. We didn't have to strive to earn God's love; it was already ours. That truth changed everything.

One thing was clear: we wanted more of God. We had seen Him move in our lives, in our marriage, and in our finances, but we knew there was so much more. I couldn't get enough. I wanted nothing more than to deepen my relationship with Jesus on a new level. Finding this place was such a divine appointment in our lives. We will always be eternally grateful to God for both this special place and our pastors who loved us so much.

Sometimes, the most stressful, challenging, and painful

situations in life are not really about that moment, but about realizing you can't do it on your own. They're about understanding that when we try to make our own decisions without Him, there are consequences. They're about discovering that He is faithful and will always be there to lift us up when we are ready to return to Him. He's ready for you too.

After our son was born in August 1994, we officially decided we were done having kids, and I had a tubal ligation. I had just turned 22, and our quiver was full and sometimes a bit chaotic. But we had each other, and most importantly, we had God!

We moved into a lovely three-bedroom rental house. It was just outside of town, but it had a beautiful yard and large rooms for the kids to play in. I remember having so much fun with them. They were all under 5 years old at the time. We were busy potty training, learning to swim, reading lots of books, and growing closer to each other and to God.

We still didn't have much, but we had each other.
And we had God, and that was enough.

Gerard worked full-time and was out of town for several weeks at a time, returning home on weekends. Often, I felt like a single mom managing our schedule, but it worked out, and I was grateful to have the freedom to stay home with our kids. I loved being with them and raising them in the truth. We still didn't have much, but we had each other. And we had God, and that was enough.

One day, I came home to find our front door open and our house broken into. It was an unsettling moment because Gerard was out of town, and I was alone with the kids at home. They stole his recording equipment from our garage, raided our piggy banks, broke some mirrors and other items while looking for valuables, and then left. We are blessed not to have been at home, and I am forever grateful for God's covering. I was a bit shaken up, so I called the police, and they arrived quickly. When the police had left, I started cleaning up and called our pastor.

I'll never forget the day he visited. He prayed for us with the kids, and we all stood in a circle praying for peace in our home. Gerard was able to come home early from work, and we told our landlord what had happened. The next day, they called and said we would need to find another place to live because they were planning to move back into their home.

God told me to tell Him what I wanted. He said to make a list and be specific.

We didn't know what we would do or where we would live, but I started praying and asking God about it. I went outside, walking and praying on the driveway, when I felt a stirring in my heart.

God told me to tell Him what I wanted. He said to make a list and be specific. He wanted to bless us. We didn't know it at the time, but this next house project would help us strengthen our faith muscles like never before.

We were heading into summer. Our oldest daughter had finished kindergarten, and the other two were three and nearly two. We met with a couple at our church who helped us create a budget a few months earlier. We were doing well and starting to save some money, but we didn't have nearly enough to buy our first home.

God Makes the Impossible Possible

We were so grateful, the couple from our church shared what we would need for this to work. They told us we needed at least $5000 down, an owner-finance option, and a miracle from God. In the natural, it looked impossible, but they encouraged us to trust God and see what He would do. We knew it would be a miracle, but we focused our faith on what God had put explicitly on my heart. So, the search for our new home began.

In the meantime, we were truly blessed to hear many different men and women of God visit our church from all over and teach us about faith. One of these mighty men of God was named Keith Moore. We will never forget his message. It has been almost thirty years, but I will cherish it in my heart forever. He was talking about surrendering those things in your life that hinder God's true blessing.

At the end of the message, he told everyone to write down what they needed from their heavenly account and ask God to do it. So, that's what we did! We wrote down on a little piece of paper to bring us at least $5000 from our heavenly account so we could purchase our first home.

We had no evidence that we could buy our first home except what God had placed on my heart. I'm sure some people probably thought we were crazy to believe we could buy a home with no cash, limited or bad credit, and not enough to furnish a house. But when you have God Almighty on your side, He is all you need!

I'm convinced that God is eager to show Himself strong on your behalf. He wants to bless His children and is looking for someone to be a blessing to. Keith Moore's message remains as true for you today as it was all those years ago. God wants to bless you, but you must let Him take the lead. You need to obey and surrender. You must believe in His power to deliver a miracle.

His Word Transforms Everything

We were so grateful to be in a place where we were hearing

truth from the Word of God and learning how to apply it to our lives. It was transforming everything. It was changing how we spoke, how we raised our children, our work ethic, and every part of our lives.

The search for our first home began. At first, we were so young, in our early 20s, and not on the same page about what we wanted. He wanted one thing, and I preferred another. He thought we could

afford a nice mobile home, and there's nothing wrong with that, but deep inside, I knew God wanted more for us. God told me to trust Him with the list I made. I did that, so why would He ask me to do that and then not be willing to provide that list?

Her tiny faith carried great weight, and we were not going to voice what seemed impossible.

When we told the kids what we were believing God for with the house, Kayla said, "We want a stairs house like Kimberlyn's." We both looked at each other and said, "Okay, let's believe God for it." Of course, in that moment, it looked impossible, and, naturally speaking, there weren't many two-story homes built in the city we lived in, but that's what she wanted. Her tiny faith carried great weight, and we were not going to voice what seemed impossible.

We had already witnessed how powerful our words were. We believed that we could have what we say, so we wanted to stay in the place of faith. So, we held our tongues and stood right there, praying for a stairs house together! You are a witness to how God gives power to our words, too.

I realize you might not fully understand God's incredible work in this season of our lives, but please keep reading. I've experienced this firsthand. It's real. God's power is real for you too, but you have to believe. This isn't about religion. The power we have because of what Jesus did is real. It's an experience I've had, and no one can take that away from me. I've lived it, and that's why it's so important to share it with you.

I want to be clear that buying our first home wasn't our idea.
It was God's.

You see, God showed us through that experience that He is a big God. He can do impossible things, and He has consistently demonstrated that to us over the years. His love is genuine, and it never fails. I want to be clear that buying our first home wasn't our idea; it was God's.

When God places something on your heart, you must believe and keep believing for it to come to pass. Many people have been confused because they ask for things God hasn't told them to believe for, and then they think God doesn't come through for them. That is not true. Of course, He can do exceedingly above whatever you can ask or think, but you need to understand that it is His will for your life, too. His Word is His will. If you're unsure of what His will is for your life, look in His Word.

He is waiting for someone to be brave enough to trust Him.

If God puts something on your heart, pursue it and learn more about what He wants to do in your life. He desires to bless His

children. I've always known Him to be kind, loving, gentle, compassionate, interested in the details of our lives, and faithful to His Word. There is nothing He cannot do. He is waiting for someone brave enough to trust Him. He is a good God. He cannot be anything but good. His Word is full of examples of this truth, and the more you explore it, the more you will see this to be true.

So here we were, believing for the impossible. The time came for us to move out of our house, and we hadn't yet found what we were looking for, so we moved in with some friends at our church. We were searching, and so were many of our friends. It felt like a faith adventure for all of us! It was so inspiring, and I loved the community around us. We were all expecting God to show up, and you will be in awe of how He did show up.

Chapter 7: A Stairs House

You can ask for anything in my name, and I will do it, so that the Son can bring glory to the Father.
John 14:13 NLT

Faith is believing without understanding everything. Faith is seeking in His Name. Faith is trusting that He will stay faithful, for your good and His glory. Faith is the heart of my story. I pray faith will be the heart of your story.

Gerard and I had talked on the way home from the amazing message delivered by Keith Moore that night. The message was monumental and life-changing for us. I was surprised when he told me, "The Lord put it on my heart to give away my recording equipment."

I may be a little ahead of myself. You may wonder whether that was the same recording equipment that was stolen during our house burglary. It was. The police had come, and we filed a report. The officers weren't very confident about recovering what was stolen, but we didn't believe that for a second. We said God would restore what was taken. And guess what? Yes, He did. We got all his studio equipment back, and it was still in working order. Unheard of for a robbery. God is faithful!

So, back to our car ride home from church. Gerard said the Lord put it on his heart to give away what we received! You need to understand how meaningful this really was. My husband has always enjoyed writing cool lyrics and catchy beats. It was more than a hobby; he loved making music. For God to tell him to give this away was a big deal. Telling me was just as important. He knew I would remind him to obey God, and of course, I did. God also directed him to whom it should be given, and he said he would call him the next day. I looked at him and said, "You know you can't do that," so I encouraged him to do it as soon as we got home. He did, and I was thrilled! God was at work.

When God Shows Off

The next morning, he went to work while I stayed home with the kids as usual. It was a typical day at the Montenegro house when I received a call from someone at our church. He had been at the service the night before with Keith Moore. He told me that at the end of the service, the Lord laid it on his heart to give us $10,000 to put toward the down payment on our new home, which we had been believing God for. He said this wasn't a loan but a gift, and when we found our home, he would be there with the check. I almost lost it right then and there! I couldn't stop laughing and crying because I knew God had answered a prayer and Gerard's obedience had opened the door for this blessing. I was so excited!

I paged my husband 911, which meant I needed to talk to him right now! Yes, I said paged him because this was before cell phones, LOL! He called me concerned, and I asked him if he was sitting down. I told him about the blessing, and he was almost speechless. We were so excited and knew this was no coincidence, and God was about to show off how good He truly is!

We kept believing and searching for our house until one day, my friend called and said, "Girl, I found your house." We went to see it and fell in love. It was exactly what we had prayed for—more expensive side of town, safe neighborhood, the right amount of space, a beautiful, fenced yard, upgrades inside and out, owner-finance, hardwood floors, a split-level plan, payment would be under $500 a month, AND it was a stairs house.

Now we needed the favor to kick in and help us close the deal!

We had everything ready for closing day except for the needed funds. We required a total of $13,100. I know, it's a steal these days. We were promised a $10,000 gift and managed to save $1,000 by living with our friends. Before we moved out of the house that was broken into, our sweet little neighbor, who must have been in her 80s, blessed us with $1,000 to help us find a new home.

She was the sweetest little old lady and had many cats. She lived alone, aside from her furry friends, and never married or had children. When we first moved into the house, she didn't like us. I believe it was because he was black and I was white, but we always showed her kindness. We would talk to her when she was outside, and the kids were playing in the front yard on their bikes and with their toys. Over time, we developed a friendship. I'm not sure how it started, but I would help her with her budget. She was very grateful for my help. One day, she came over and I told her we were going to have to move because we were trying to buy our own house, and she wanted to help us. Later, she came back with a $1,000 check. I was stunned. God used my sweet little neighbor, who didn't even like us at first when we moved in, to bless us.

We paused, prayed, and asked God what to do!

Closing day had arrived. We were $1,100 short of the needed amount. The man who was blessing us with the $10,000 called to see if everything was still on track. We told him it was, even though we knew we were short. We were literally trusting God! We paused, prayed, and asked God what to do! We called our pastor and asked him to pray.

We told him our position on the faith project, and he asked how much we still needed. I said $1,000. He said, 'We'll give it to you!' We were stunned! Oh, my goodness! What was God doing?! I just blurted out $1,000 because I knew we had a couple of hundred dollars in our savings account, and I could use that to cover the remaining $100.

We stopped by and picked up the last $1,000 we needed, and I dropped off the kids with a close friend. She was going to watch them while we closed on our first house. She asked how it was going, and I told her we got everything we needed! She was so excited because they believed with us for this house, along with many of our wonderful friends from church. Then she said that God must really want to bless us and handed me an envelope. I smiled, hugged her, and said thank you.

When I got in the car, I planned to quickly run to the bank for the remaining money we needed. But first, I opened the envelope, and wow, guess what was inside. Yes! A $100 bill was inside. I couldn't stop laughing and crying happy tears! I still feel the overwhelming joy and the sense of God's love and favor that surrounded me at that moment.

I believe that God truly wants to be a blessing to His kids,
But he is waiting for us to ask for big things!

We closed that day and moved our family into our new-to-us house with stairs. We remained the same physically, but our faith grew tremendously through this faith project. We quickly started furnishing our home, and God continued to bless our efforts. We never stopped paying our tithe, and we always believed for increase so we could give more. We weren't wealthy financially, but we had everything we needed. The kids loved their new rooms, and our yard was beautiful. Big, stunning oak trees shaded the front and back yards, with the lushest green St. Augustine grass. All of those were items on my list, too. I believe that God truly wants to be a blessing to His kids, but He is waiting for us to ask for big things!

Ask and You Shall Receive

The Bible says, "We have not because we ask not." This means we don't receive what we want or need because we aren't asking Him for it. He is a good God who only wants to provide well for His children. We've never known God to withhold blessings, giving us not only what we need but also what we want. He gave us what my five-year-old daughter and her three-year-old sister requested—a stairs house! What seemed completely impossible was not only possible but likely, not just because of our faith, but because He wants to bless His kids!

Will you let Him bless you, too?

The stairs house is where we both realized that we are called to ministry. It holds a very special place in our hearts. Gerard was away at a men's conference when he received the call. I was simply at home taking care of the kids. Every day, I followed the same routine. Once I put the kids down for a nap, I would spend time worshiping God and just seeking Him. I was so hungry for more of God and wanted to know Him more intimately than the day before.

There was so much peace and joy in that place.

This is when I saw that He wanted to use me in worship. I always loved to sing, and God had delivered me from the fear of being in front of people. Now I realize how valuable and refreshing it was to worship God for who He is. This is also when I began journaling regularly and writing down the things God would show me in that secret place of His presence. There was so much peace and joy there. I came to love it more than anything in the world. I never wanted to leave that place. I would tell the Lord that, and one day He said to me that I didn't have to leave His presence. He told me that His presence was in me and would always be with me. I know that sounds very simple, but it was profound to me to hear that I could literally live in this place of peace, joy, and surrender.

He expanded my understanding of who He was, how vast His love for me was, and that He only wanted me to live in that kind of love. This is also where I built upon the foundation of God's love. His love never fails, and He would show me a picture of me sitting in His lap, wrapped up in His love. He was healing me from the inside out, and it was so beautiful.

Seek Him in prayer and worship. Feel His joy as you spend more time in His presence. Make Him a part of every part of your day. Believe in His desire to provide for you, seek to understand what He wants to do for you, and stand firm in your faith as He delivers far more than you thought you could ask for. God wants to be with His children, and you are His child. God never calls us His adults. He's so good.

"The Stairs House"

Chapter 8: This is Your Healing

Then your light shall break forth like the morning, Your healing shall spring forth speedily, And your righteousness shall go before you; The glory of the Lord shall be your rear guard. Isaiah 58:8 NKJV

In that moment, the Lord said, "This is your healing."

There's nothing quite like trusting God for a miracle. It's special, breathtaking, and soul-stirring. When that moment comes, when He draws you in and speaks directly to your heart, you know you'll never be the same. That's when He said to me, "This is your healing."

We moved into our house at the end of the summer in 1996. We had been married for six years, had three kids who were 6, 3, and 2 at that time, and they kept us very busy. We were connected to a wonderful church, actively serving, and we loved our life. Although not perfect, our marriage was still a bit crazy at times because we were so young, and managing three kids at just 24 years old was a lot. But God is so good, and He kept blessing us with favor and provision every step of the way.

We were now homeowners, and God was just getting warmed up. I felt blessed to get a part-time job working at our church's academy, where Kayla started 1st grade. It was perfect for our family. I taught music and drama. I led worship for chapel days during the week. I was so happy to be working with kids and doing what I love—worship! It was an excellent place for me to keep growing and learning.

I was singing in the choir and on the worship team, and I also wrote and recorded radio announcements and prayers for the station. At that time, our church owned a radio station in town. I don't remember exactly how that opportunity came into my life, but I remember loving it deeply. Writing these blurbs sparked my passion for creative thinking and putting my thoughts on paper. The revelation God gave me during this period was incredible, especially since my children were so young. I learned so much just by being with them, watching them grow, and seeing how they developed their faith.

Recently, I found some of my notes from that time, and they took me back to when our son, Gee, was just 2½ years old. We had Gospel Duck (Len Mink) come to our church one Sunday night to minister. When we walked into the church, all of his materials were for sale in the foyer. My son picked out a video he really wanted and asked me, "Mommy, buy that for me?" I replied, "Mommy can't right now, but let's pray for it." We did just that right there. He kneeled and said, "Thank You, Jesus, for my video, Amen," and then the kids went to their classes.

That night, they saw their faith in action!

After the service, someone approached my husband and handed him the entire package of videos and cassettes. About a week earlier, my children had blessed others with some videos and cassettes. We always taught our children that it was important to sow seeds of giving to others, not to get something in return, but to be a blessing. We told them that God would always bless them for being generous. That night, they saw their faith in action! When Gerard picked up Gee from his class and saw the videos, he said, "Daddy, you buy these for me," and Gerard replied, "No, son, God blessed you with these." He said, "Wow!"

The Wedding We Never Had

Not long after, someone blessed us with $1,000 to buy me a new wedding ring set. When we eloped, we didn't have much money for a nice set. Our 8th anniversary was coming up, so since God blessed us with that money, we decided to buy me a new ring and renew our wedding vows with our pastor. He was excited to do this for us, and we were too!

Gerard asked me during our anniversary week what I would want if we could do something special. Of course, I wanted my parents to be there, and for it to feel like a wedding I never had, but he assured me it was best to keep it just between us. I argued a little and said we had already done that, but I finally agreed. I did tell him it would be nice to have music since we both loved music so much. He said Okay.

It was a beautiful Saturday morning in Florida—slightly brisk, but the sky was perfectly clear. January 31, 1998, had arrived, marking the perfect day for a wedding, which was our anniversary. The plan was for him to meet me at the church since he had a few errands to run beforehand. My friends were coming over to stay with the kids, so it would be an intimate ceremony. Still, we both had a renewed faith in our hearts.

I arrived at the church wearing the dark green formal dress I had chosen, and my friend greeted me at the side entrance. I didn't know she would be there, but she encouraged me to follow her, so

I did. We walked into the church and into one of the kids' classrooms, where she opened the door to reveal a beautiful white wedding dress hanging up, along with white shoes and a stunning veil. I was speechless, which doesn't happen very often! What was going on?

Her husband was there and recorded my reaction, which I still enjoy watching today. They didn't tell me everything that was planned but said I needed to get changed and ready for what was next. I was a willing participant in this plan even though I had no idea what they were talking about. I hadn't received the memo about this change! I walked out still thinking I was going to our pastor's office to meet Gerard for our renewal ceremony when she told me to turn left toward the front doors.

I turned around and saw a sharply dressed gentleman in a black suit, bowtie, and cummerbund holding the door open for me. Under the portico was a beautiful white Cadillac with a navy-blue top. I felt just like Cinderella being hurried off to the ball by her little friends! Again, I was a willing participant in this plan and hopped into the car. By now, I couldn't stop crying, laughing, and smiling, but I was trying hard not to let my makeup run down my face! My friend was right there to wipe away my happy tears and told me she would see me later.

My chauffeur, who was also one of our close friends, wouldn't reveal the plan to me because he had sworn to secrecy, but he asked if I wanted a mint. I know this story might seem like a dream, as if it never really happened, but it did. I have the video, pictures, and my family and friends to prove it. I've always dreamed of my wedding since I was a little girl. I wanted to be like Cinderella in a big, beautiful dress, feel special, and have my Daddy walk me down the aisle to give me away to my Prince Charming. How many of you can relate?

I had been tricked into the most beautiful and pleasant surprise of my life—a wedding!

We drove out of town to a beautiful, peaceful spot called Chandler. A family from our church owned a lovely piece of property with a small lake. There was a gazebo that extended over the water. When we arrived, I saw some of our friends, beautiful flowers, and our pastor in the gazebo, which had a large pink sign that said, "I love you, Rolanda." I had been tricked into the most beautiful and joyful surprise of my life—a wedding! The one I didn't get to have but always wanted. I just knew God was winking at me.

As we sat in the car for a moment, I watched my husband arrive with our three babies following behind him—all dressed to the nines! He was wearing a black tuxedo with tails and a top hat, and our girls looked stunning in their dresses, while our son was in his little suit. I was in awe of this moment, and every time I share this story, I can't help but cry. It was probably one of the most breathtaking moments of my life. I could have stayed there forever.

It was time for me to get out of the car, and my friend was there to wipe my face again, removing the tears that kept flowing down my cheeks. I wondered where my dad was, and then, as I stepped out, I found him. He had been hiding behind a tree with my bouquet in his hand, tears in his eyes, and he gave me one of the biggest hugs. In that moment, the Lord said, "This is your healing." We cried, hugged, and then cried some more. He told me he loved me, and those words went deeper than ever before.

My dream, which I thought would never come true, finally did.

After a few minutes, it was time for him to walk me down the aisle. My dream, which I thought would never come true, finally did. I absorbed every moment like a sponge as we shared this special time, just daddy and me. As we reached the gazebo, everyone had tears in their eyes. Many of our friends knew our testimony and understood how meaningful this moment truly was for us. I was thankful to share it with them. My mom, Gerard's parents, and all three of our children were in the gazebo too. Of course, my dear friends from the church worship team, who sang with me, were there and performed the most beautiful songs at our wedding. Gerard gave me music and so much more.

God Ideas

My husband had everything planned, and I believe he was hearing from God. We like to call them 'God ideas.' He received the idea and miraculously pulled it off in just three days. We saw God's favor in every detail. When his employer found out what he was planning, they wanted to help, so they paid for all the flowers. The property owners didn't charge us anything and made sure the grounds were perfect for our day. Our friends helped Gerard rent his tuxedo, and his sister kindly let me borrow her wedding dress. Of course, they had no idea if it would fit me, but it fit like a glove. Our pastor was there, and we were so blessed that he could marry us on such short notice. Everyone worked together and arranged a small reception afterward so we could enjoy cake. To top it all off, they blessed us with a night in a nice hotel, just the two of us.

Daddy walking me down the aisle.

Our little family.
January 31, 1998

Just before our anniversary, we faced struggles in our marriage. We were complete opposites in many ways because of how we met. We had to learn to be friends. We jumped into intimacy too quickly, making it the focus early on, and our communication was poor. We grew up very differently, which also created challenges, but we were determined to stay together no matter what.

Our renewal was a reset for us. It gave me the chance to see a side of my husband I had never seen before. He showed me how much he truly listened to what mattered to me by making sure my dad was there to walk me down the aisle. Afterwards, my dad shared at the reception with everyone that I had called him the day before, and I apologized that he wouldn't get to be there, but we would celebrate with him, my mom, and everyone afterward. On the phone, he stayed calm and didn't give in to my concerns or spill Gerard's plan. My dad said it was so hard because he didn't want me to be upset, but he trusted Gerard, and that was a big deal. Gerard assured him that I would be okay, and everything would be better if I were surprised.

The number eight holds deep meaning for me because of the special day we shared, and because of its symbolism. I will tell another God story about the number eight later in this book. "New Beginnings" is what the number eight represents. On January 31, 1998, God gave us a fresh start. When I hugged my dad and heard the Lord speak those words into my heart, I knew we would never be the same, and we weren't.

Will you go to God? Will you give Him your heart? Will you trust Him to fulfill the dreams you never thought were possible? Will you allow Him to give you a fresh start? If you do, I promise you will never be the same.

Chapter 9: The Call

Pray in the Spirit at all times and on every occasion. Stay alert and be persistent in your prayers for all believers everywhere.
Ephesians 6:18 NLT

We knew God wasn't short on money, and all we needed was enough faith to believe God for what we needed. So that's what we did. Naturally, or rather supernaturally, God came through beyond our wildest expectations!

Fresh from a whirlwind wedding on our eighth anniversary, we continued to grow in our faith. We were both sensing a calling to ministry. Growing up as a PK, ministry was never on my wish list. In fact, as a teenager, I proudly declared I would never be a pastor's wife. HA! God was probably laughing every time I said that. He knew what He had planned for me. He knew I would submit to Him. Still, He had a good laugh at my expense, over and over.

Visions of a Church

God showed me visions of us having a church while we were still in the late 90s. That vision would take nearly twenty years to develop. The calling was stronger in Gerard, so he felt called to start a Bible Training correspondence course. He would work on it for a few months, then get distracted by life and other things. He also felt like he wasn't getting what he needed from it. He thought that he needed more.

He told us to list all the pros and cons and then pray in the Spirit about it.

During that time, an opportunity for ministry arose for us to move to another city further south. We visited the place, and surprisingly, we were both offered excellent jobs. But something inside didn't feel right. Gerard talked to our pastor, and he gave us some of the best advice. He told us to list all the pros and cons and then pray in the Spirit about it. Relying on our own understanding was not reliable, but praying in the Spirit would help us discover God's perfect will for our lives. That's exactly what it did.

The Lord showed us that it wasn't the right time to move physically, but rather to deepen our connection with Him and press into Him even more. Essentially, God wanted us to move inward, not outward. Finding peace in His presence and purpose, we pressed into God. We read our Bibles, attended church whenever there was a service, went to conferences to strengthen our faith, served consistently, and gave faithfully. We genuinely desired everything God had for us, including a stronger relationship with each other.

This was a significant step of faith!

Both of our jobs reached a point where further advancement required more education in our field. However, neither of us felt called to remain in our current roles. We knew we were meant for ministry, so we began seeking God's guidance. He strongly impressed upon us to move to Broken Arrow, OK, and attend Rhema Bible Training Center. This was a significant step of faith!

Once again, we talked to our pastor and asked him to pray with us for clear guidance on what God wanted us to do. We waited and prayed. Meanwhile, we also planned our first mission trip together. Our church was sending a large team to Honduras to help build a pastor's home, which would serve multiple purposes in the area. We were fundraising for this, but we also felt called to go to Rhema. Would God have us do both? Why not?

We were able to go on our mission trip to Honduras, and it was such a blessing to serve the people, see their hunger for the Lord, and help build a new house for the pastor. I discovered that I really enjoy making things, especially hammering nails! Haha! I also connected with some of the ladies at the school there and was able to encourage them, since I had been a teacher at the academy for about three years by then. I was asked to sing and speak at the services our team held. It was a life-changing experience I will never forget. My only wish is that we could have taken our kids with us, but they were too young at the time.

We still needed some money to come in before we could move, but we knew God was in this decision, so we felt confident we would have what we needed.

Once we decided to move to Oklahoma, we also chose to sell our house. Our realtor, who was part of our church, was such a blessing. We applied for school, and everything looked promising for us to move in August, just before the kids would start school. Our oldest daughter would be in 4th grade, our middle daughter in 1st, and our youngest son would begin kindergarten. We found an apartment complex near the school and secured our new three-bedroom apartment. We still needed some money to come in before we could move, but we knew God was in this decision, so we felt confident we would have what we needed when we needed it.

A New Assignment

The moment finally arrived for us to move, and our pastor prayed a prayer of blessing over us during our last service. It was so beautiful, and although we would miss our church family, we understood the assignment God had given us.

The next morning, we were ready to leave, but our car wouldn't start. We called a mechanic and had it repaired. Meanwhile, the truck was packed, with only a few items left in the house—some pillows, blankets, a phone, and our answering machine. When we returned after dropping off the car, we received a message from a man we didn't know. Gerard had submitted one job application in Broken Arrow, and from that single application, he received a call from the company's president. He returned the call, had a phone interview, and got the job—earning $4 more an hour than before! We were so happy! Instead of stressing over the car trouble, we decided to trust God and see what He would do, keeping a positive attitude. I'm thankful we did because we would have missed that call if the car hadn't broken down that morning! God is so good, and He knows everything! His love never fails, and His timing is always perfect!

I hope you are sensing the magnitude of what this story is supposed to mean to you. An unexpected pregnancy eventually gives way to a beautiful wedding. Racial challenges from family that gave way to a lifelong marriage, three amazing kids, and a heart for Jesus. Obedience to the will of God gave way to unthinkable joy in His calling, unwavering love in His arms, and blessings beyond comprehension in His service.

The circumstances may be completely different for you, or not much at all. The blessings will be yours, specially prepared for you, and are waiting for your willingness to accept them. Even when your car breaks down, God is there. Oh, and if you declare you will never do something in His service, just know that if it's in His plans for you, He will laugh. And you will thank Him for it.

Gerard's new job and pay raise meant I could stay home with the kids and didn't need to look for extra income. We were so excited! The next day, we drove out full of faith, speaking over our house to sell in Jesus' name. We were still walking this out in faith!

We learned that once you pray and ask God for what you need or want, you should thank Him for it.

Until that point, we didn't receive much interest from people in our house, but we understood the power of our words and kept speaking that it was sold even after we left. God gave us that house to begin with, and we knew He would help us sell it to the right family. We just had to be patient and watch Him work it out.

We learned that once you pray and ask God for what you need or want, you should thank Him for it. There's no need to keep asking or begging Him to do it; trust and believe that it is already done! This has been key in building our faith and teaching our kids as well. They saw us do this consistently and watched God come through for our family repeatedly. I am so thankful for this journey of faith that God has us on, and even now, He still guides us along this path. I wouldn't want it any other way. Until we all get to heaven, we will always have adventures in faith, as I like to call them.

In the end, we helped pay for the registration of the very family that was older and more well-off than we were.

When we arrived in Oklahoma, we managed to pay for our registration and book fees, and the best part was that we could also help someone else! This was a true testimony! Some people close to us thought it might not be the right time for us to move across the country with our small family and take such a big leap of faith. They compared our journey to another family who was a bit more financially stable and slightly older than us, and who also moved to Oklahoma to attend Bible school. We were surprised, and if I'm being honest, a little disappointed by this, but we knew that God had told us exactly what we needed to do, so we trusted that God would provide. In the end, we helped pay for the registration of the very family that was older and more well-off than we were. God is worthy of our trust. If He tells you to do something, you can be sure He will never fail you. He doesn't fail. Love never fails.

This is the main reason you need to hear from God yourself. I understand that people mean well; they genuinely do, but often they are afraid that things won't work out for you and speak out of fear rather than faith. You must recognize the difference. You are responsible for hearing from God on your own. The good news is that He is not hiding His will from you. He wants to reveal His plan for your life; you only need to be willing to spend time with Him to discover it. There's so much joy in that.

Hearing God's Voice

Hearing God's voice isn't impossible; in fact, God wants to communicate with us. We often get so busy that we forget to take the time to listen. Just a few minutes in the morning with God can change your entire day. There's no substitute for spending time with Him. You get to know Him by spending time with Him, and you recognize His voice by listening. It's like having a friend—the more time you spend with them, the easier it is to recognize their voice when they call. The same is true with God. His voice is the most important one you will ever hear, so why not set aside some time to become more familiar with it? He loves you so much and wants to have a real relationship with you. I pray you will truly know and experience His love for you through every word in this book.

The kids started at their new school, and we began Bible School. We were following our calling. During this time, we still believed our home would sell. While we were away during the first month, our realtor kindly paid for our rent. The very next month, our house sold! We were excited to see God come through, and we received everything we needed from the sale of our home.

On one occasion, we sat in a class talking to a kind older woman who shared that she had been in a car accident and had totaled her vehicle. She was spending all her money on renting a car. She really needed another vehicle but couldn't afford one. Over the years, several people had given us cars, and we always said we couldn't wait to do the same for someone else.

For several years, we prayed for a minivan. I rewrote the lyrics to a song for my kids and me to sing, thanking God for our minivan. "Thank You, Lord, for our minivan…" I still remember the melody today, over thirty years later. Haha! I bet my kids can sing it too! We had no idea how we could afford to give someone a car, but we wanted to do it and asked God to help us. And He did!

"Faith says thank you!"

One of the things our pastor always said was "Faith says thank you!" That stuck with me, and we realized that gratitude played a big role in everything we did and how we lived our lives. After we prayed and asked God for a minivan, we decided to start thanking Him for it. Of course, we didn't get a minivan overnight, but we kept believing and thanking God for it, even when we didn't see any changes.

When that kind lady in class shared her heartfelt story about trusting for a breakthrough with her car situation, my husband and I looked at each other, knowing exactly what the other was thinking. Once we received our check from selling the house, we were able to buy our minivan in cash! Hallelujah!

The next day, we couldn't wait to give that lady our car keys, and when we did, she was so blessed! God is so good, and He wants to bless you so you can be a blessing to others. We are living proof of this throughout our lives, and I bet you have similar stories of how good He truly is. You don't have to have everything figured out or live perfectly for God to use you; you just need to be willing and available.

The revelation God poured into our hearts was profound.

We spent two years in Broken Arrow, OK, as we received our certificate from Rhema Bible Training Center in May 2001. Both of our parents came to celebrate this special occasion with us.

During our time there, we grew significantly, and God began to broaden our vision. Often at Rhema Bible Church, Pastor Hagin would pray over people as they were sent out to various parts of the world to share the Gospel. It was such an inspiring experience to be there at that time. It was also an honor and privilege to learn under such anointed teaching, especially from the late Brother Kenneth E. Hagin. The revelation God poured into our hearts was profound, and we will always cherish this meaningful time in our lives.

While we were at Rhema, we connected with a missionary from Africa. He called us one day when he was in town and asked us to join him for dinner. We felt honored by the invitation and met with him. He mentioned having a dream about us and expressed interest in helping him start another church in Zimbabwe. We had never considered this before, but we were definitely open to whatever God might have in store for us.

The Value of Spiritual Covering

We contacted our pastor in Florida about it, and once again, he offered us valuable advice. He said, "That's a new thought, let me pray about this." He prayed, then reached out to us with an internship offer at our home church in Ocala. This opportunity would focus on ministry, giving us the chance to experience each department firsthand through hands-on learning. They offered me a position in the office, and Gerard could intern during the week whenever his schedule allowed, outside of his full-time job. God blessed him with the ability to work from home for the same company in Oklahoma when we moved back to Ocala, FL. We felt complete peace about this decision and recognized it as the Lord's wisdom not to move across the world. We were open, but I'm so grateful we connected with our pastor. Having spiritual covering is so important. We will always be thankful for them.

We returned in 2001 and stayed engaged until summer 2005. During this period, we learned a lot, which prepared us to eventually start our own church. We participated in various church departments, gaining insight into every area of church leadership. From administration to the children's department, from the care team to the media ministry, and much more. Our hearts were full, and we were eager to learn and serve.

During this time, God laid it on my heart to record a worship CD. One of my dear friends helped us complete this wonderful project. She is also the one assisting me again as I write my first book. I felt so blessed to return to Rhema and record at their studio with the worship leader, who has since gone to heaven. What a great experience, and I learned a lot. God was opening doors for me to travel locally and lead worship at women's conferences and Christian concert events, and it was truly amazing!

Things seemed stable, but I lacked peace about moving forward.

Along with Gerard's internship at the church, he was also attending nearby church-planting conferences. Our kids were busy at school, playing sports, and making friends. Gerard and I weren't on the same page about when to start a church. He wanted to do it then, but I knew we weren't ready for such a big step yet. Our communication needed improvement, and we were still relatively young, raising our family. Things seemed stable, but I lacked peace about moving forward. So, we didn't. Instead, we chose to support one of our associate pastors with a church plant in Chicago.

God placed it on our hearts to sell our house, take the proceeds, and dedicate three months to supporting the pastors with whatever they needed. Once again, we were obedient. We learned and grew from the experience. Living in a colder climate was tough, and I didn't enjoy driving in the snow. During that time, we met some wonderful people, but we knew it was only a temporary move. By then, we had a child in high school, another in middle school, and our son was in his last year of elementary school.

In some ways, we rushed this move. We were getting antsy about our situation and felt a bit stuck. Impatience can be dangerous. We were in our early 30s and thinking we were already falling behind. The devil is so pushy and makes everyone feel that way once you reach that decade. Thinking you are "behind" can throw you off balance and cause you to miss the right timing, which is not a good thing.

The Power of Restoration

The good news is that God is powerful enough to fix anything you mess up and still work things out for your good. We loved God and committed ourselves to following Him. Moving to Chicago taught us a lot about starting a church from scratch, but eventually we realized it was time for something different, even though we weren't exactly sure what that was.

We did pray, but our hearts were already set on going, so we went.

As the school year was coming to an end, we sought God's guidance. We had friends who started a church in Texas. We visited and fell in love with the people and the place. I preferred a warmer climate too; growing up in Florida was special, and I missed the sunshine. We spoke to our pastor in Florida before moving to Texas, and he advised us to pray about it but told us he didn't think it was wise. We did pray, but our hearts were already set on going, so we went.

I'm sharing this because I want you to realize that we haven't always followed good advice. We learned an important lesson through this process, and it's vital to understand that every choice has consequences. We may not always agree with our pastors, and we might think we know better, but if someone in your life is willing to tell you the truth—especially if it's something you don't want to hear or don't understand now—you should still respect their voice in your life. They're not perfect either, but God grants them wisdom, and sometimes they know things you don't.

We moved to Texas and spent nearly ten years there, serving faithfully and growing spiritually. We both served on staff at one point, but it was probably the most toxic environment we've ever experienced. Despite the positive experiences we had with our pastor in Florida, we now faced the complete opposite in many ways. It took us a decade to realize this, but once the blinders were removed, it became clear we needed to move on.

Gerard and I have often said we learned a lot about ministry, especially what not to do.

I know many people have gone through church hurt over the years, and it's real. We've experienced it too, but I love the church. God established it, and He said that the gates of hell would not prevail against it (Matthew 16:18). That's serious. Gerard and I have often said we learned a lot about ministry, especially what not to do.

It's always easier to criticize leadership when you're not the one in charge. We've fallen into this trap before, and I want to encourage you not to repeat it. I believe the enemy wants us to criticize others so we become distracted and are not used by God to pray for them. We must remember that no one is perfect. Just because God calls you to ministry, to teach a class, pastor a church, evangelize the lost, lead worship, or go on the mission field, that doesn't mean you're exempt from fighting the same spiritual battles as everyone else. Often, you're fighting an even bigger battle because the enemy hates what you're doing, and he will use anything to come against you, even Christians.

Overcoming Fear Again

During this time, I realized the benefits of living free from fear, rejection, and condemnation. I am genuinely grateful for the revelation God gave me to help me let go of condemnation. I was so focused on trying to please others that I didn't see that God was already pleased with me just because I believe in Him. I will always hold this truth close to my heart.

One of the best books my dad encouraged Gerard and me to read when we started in ministry is called "The Way of the Shepherd" by Kevin Leman and William Pentak. I highly recommend this book to everyone, especially those who care for others. He said, "What distinguishes a great leader from a mediocre one is that a great leader has a heart for his people." (Leman/Pentak, pg. 101) Having a heart for others is fundamental to any leadership, and if you don't have it, eventually you won't have anyone following you.

God sees and knows, and He can heal your broken heart.

I am by no means excusing the pain caused by any leader; I acknowledge that it's real. I've experienced it myself, and I'm sure I've caused some, too. I am certain I have some PTSD from our last experience, but I will not let that stop me from following God's will for my life. It's tragic when people are hurt, especially by someone they trust so deeply. I have no words except that God sees and knows, and He can heal your broken heart. I know this because He has done it for me.

I pray that you will open your heart to Him, and if necessary, talk to a professional and seek help. Please, please don't suffer alone. Life is too short to stay stuck in the past or any trauma that the devil intended for you; he is truly the one responsible. Let God heal you from past hurts. He is the only One who can.

Chapter 10: Put Me In, Coach

Also I heard the voice of the Lord, saying: "Whom shall I send, And who will go for Us?" Then I said, "Here am I! Send me."
Isaiah 6:8 NKJV

After twenty years of marriage, we finally seem to have clicked. Maybe we are late bloomers, but with all the turmoil we faced when we got together, we had a long road to recovery ahead of us. I'm sure some of our decisions weren't always the right ones, which might have made it take longer to resolve issues. Thankfully, God never gives up on us. He is always there to help us move forward if we choose not to quit!

Our ten-year stay in Texas included a detour to Pennsylvania for about 18 months. Yes, another move! Once again, we stepped in to help a new pastor take charge of a church as the current pastor was retiring. We offered whatever support he needed. In Pennsylvania, we met some of the most wonderful people, and that period was very meaningful for Gerard and me. We grew more than we had in a long time because we were truly desperate. It felt like being in the desert — not literally, but it was a challenging time. That tough period brought us closer, both to each other and to the God we serve. I can honestly say that in 2010, our marriage took a positive turn.

After about 18 months in Pennsylvania, we moved back to Texas and returned to the same church. Of course, we thought it was great compared to where we had been, and we felt content. Our kids were happy to be back with their friends, and our oldest daughter had just gotten married. Life was so good.

A New Beginning

I started working for an in-house outreach program aimed at helping people learn how to manage their money and reach their goals. Blending social work and life coaching, it was the perfect fit. For the first time in a long time, I felt like I was doing something I loved and that came naturally to me. I was responsible for developing our life coach training, writing and producing our life skills university curriculum, and building this new ministry from the ground up. I was excited to take on this challenge!

I discovered a life-coaching program to earn my certification as a life coach. This transformed everything for me! I enjoyed learning. Helping people reach their goals and keeping them accountable felt very natural. I loved encouraging them and showing what was possible. Over the eleven and a half years of leading this amazing organization, I met many wonderful people.

My heart for you, as presented in these pages, reflects my calling to help people achieve their goals. It is to help people achieve freedom in Jesus Christ. It is to help people fulfill their calling. It is my prayer that you see how God works for the good of those who seek Him, and let Him help you become all He created you to be.

By now, I was in my early 40s and hadn't gone back to school since we attended Rhema, which was 14 years ago. After earning my life coaching certification, I wanted more. Not that I needed it, but something inside me truly desired it. I mentioned this to someone, and they didn't think I should pursue it, which surprised me a bit. They had their education and were very successful. I wondered why they didn't recognize it as a good fit for me too. I talked to my husband about it, and he encouraged me to go for it if that's what I wanted. So, that's what I did.

One of my close friends was a teacher, and she helped guide me through the steps to start college. I had to take a remedial math class, which I expected. But I was determined. I started school in June 2015 at nearly 43 years old. I was so excited to be learning.

I was learning, and it felt so good.

I chose communication/speech as my major after several attempts to figure it out. It made me think about how young teens just graduating high school could know what field they want to study, since it took me until age 43 to figure it out. I was learning, and it felt so good.

During my years at the nonprofit, I grew immensely as a leader. I loved coaching and helping people. We served individuals from diverse backgrounds. Some faced crises, while others just needed guidance and direction. I was challenged to help them find creative solutions. I enjoyed working with other nonprofit leaders in our community and valued the process of helping people become the best version of themselves.

Change will cost you something—comfort, time, energy, money, and significant effort.

I learned that just because people say they want to change, it doesn't always mean they are ready for it. I've been there too.

Change will cost you something—comfort, time, energy, money, and significant effort. Sometimes it may even cost you friends, family members, and other things you didn't expect. Change is hard, but it is possible, and that's what we help people understand.

Whatever God has placed in your heart to do, go and do it!

I realized that as I helped others become more consistent and discover their dreams and goals, I was also strengthening my own discipline to achieve mine. I found joy and satisfaction in assisting hundreds of people in reaching various goals over the years. From paying off debt to establishing a daily routine, from growing spiritually to returning to school for their degree, there are no stupid goals, as I would tell them. Whatever God has placed in your heart to do, go and do it! I would tell them it was possible if they were willing to do whatever it took. Many achieved incredible results.

I used to tell new clients during their intake interviews that we would discuss their past that day so I could get to know them. However, afterward, we would set it aside to focus on what was next. Sometimes, that wasn't easy, and they needed counseling or therapy to overcome their past. But they were willing to openly share their life stories with me. What an honor and privilege that was for me!

The Hope Office

I told them they were sitting in the Hope Office! I was there to inspire them to see what could be possible by taking that small step toward their dreams and goals. Nothing was impossible, and I realized many people lacked the support and encouragement needed to face even the simplest challenges. Some individuals have been so traumatized by life and torn down by family or bad relationships that they have no self-esteem.

NOT in the Hope Office. Everything changed in that room for the better. I was living in my sweet spot. Helping people in such an authentic way was like witnessing a sunset every day at the best part of the beach.

Our volunteer life coaches truly were the heroes. They dedicated time to meet with our clients, offering support, encouragement, and accountability to help them achieve their goals. It required a lot of patience and love. I learned so much from them and tried to motivate them as they motivated our clients. This is a season of my life I will always cherish. The people I was able to love, care for, and support will always hold a special place in my heart.

"Listening is the foundation for coaching."

Coaching became one of my favorite things to do and be. I love encouraging people, and maybe that's why I always wanted to be a cheerleader when I was younger. I believe that coaching has been an extension of my faith and calling, and a practical way to help people embrace real change in their lives. One of the lessons my coaching instructor said was, "Listening is the foundation for coaching." I will never forget that. Coaching freed me from feeling like I always had to have the answers, but it helped me see that if we give people space to think and speak freely without judgment, most of the time they will figure out the answers themselves. I witnessed this time and time again.

After nearly ten years at the church in Texas and experiencing a lot of heartbreak upon discovering the unthinkable, we decided to leave. It caused turmoil in our lives, but we knew we couldn't stay. God was moving and reignited in our hearts that it was time to start our own ministry.

Faith Comes Alive

In March 2016, we hosted a prayer meeting at one of our close friends' homes, and 32 people attended. A few weeks later, in April, we held our first official service. We felt truly blessed to follow God's calling. We knew this was our purpose. After years of preparing for ministry, studying at Rhema, and working with various pastors and ministries, it was finally time. We were both excited and nervous! God has blessed us with many wonderful people over the years who helped turn the vision into reality. Faith Alive Church was born, and it continues to grow strong.

If you've ever started a ministry or a business, you know it's all-consuming. My plate was overflowing with responsibilities. I was still in school, working toward my bachelor's degree, working full-time for the nonprofit, and now we had a church. Our youngest son had recently gotten married, and we only had our middle daughter still living at home. We were almost empty nesters, but we were never in a hurry. I loved having my babies around and still do!

The ministry was challenging during the first few years as we were finding our footing, and we already had just over 100 people consistently attending, sometimes exceeding 200. It was just my husband and me until 2018, when we hired our first staff member. As the stress and heaviness started to weigh heavily on me, especially physically, I noticed I was heavier than I had ever been and felt terrible. My back was always sore, my feet hurt, and although I love wearing high heels, that became more difficult with the extra weight I was carrying.

I had to do something because I was so miserable.

I tried several things. I would lose some and then gain more back. I was on a wild roller coaster, getting closer to 50. I had to do something because I was so miserable. I didn't know what, but I started looking for answers.

We were in 2020, the year the world went crazy, when I found myself stuck. My father-in-law unexpectedly passed away in March. We worked from home like the rest of the country. Of course, that didn't help when choosing healthier options. That was also the time when my husband started experimenting in the kitchen. For thirty years of our marriage, I had always done the cooking. He could make a few things, but I mostly handled all the cooking. This was so refreshing and helpful, especially as I was nearing the end of college.

People criticized our actions or inactions at church.

Many of our friends experienced significant loss and devastation because of the pandemic, and it was difficult to navigate. People criticized our actions or inactions at church. It was a reminder that you can't please everyone all the time. This was a crucial time to hear God's voice and understand His will. Some ministries, churches, and nonprofits didn't survive this unpredictable and challenging period. We felt so blessed to still minister to those who were hurting and to continue thriving as a church family. God gave us creative ways to serve, just as He did for many others around the world.

In the fall of 2020, I went for a routine checkup and mammogram. I discovered I was pre-diabetic due to my weight gain, and my cholesterol was also slightly high. That was new to me—quite unsettling—and I didn't want to be on medication for diabetes, high blood pressure, or anything else. I'm grateful for medicine, don't get me wrong; we're fortunate to live in a country where it's readily available. However, I didn't want to rely on medication for my health. The mammogram results were clear, but they advised me to do self-checks since my breasts are dense, and spotting any abnormalities might be difficult.

We welcomed our first grandbaby at the end of 2019, and she was becoming more mobile. I desperately wanted to avoid missing any of her milestones because of my health issues or inability to keep up. This meant a lot to me. I always looked forward to becoming a grandmother, as I am called, Mimi. I wanted to be there for my grandkids and enjoy them as much as I could. I knew something had to change with my health.

If you are stressed, overwhelmed, under pressure, and struggling to keep up, please know God is with you every step of the way. Seek Him in prayer and worship. Lean on Him and let Him help you bear your burdens. He is not only willing but also eager to help. It's what He does best.

Chapter 11: The One Decision That Changed Everything

O my people, trust in him at all times.
Pour out your heart to him, for God is our refuge.
Psalm 62:8 NLT

Still, I knew God had me. He's got you, too. But you have to let Him.

We met for lunch, and I'll never forget sitting there, watching her. We were approaching the end of 2020, and I had been watching my friend who had recently regained her health. She looked fantastic, and I was glad I suggested we connect.

She never once touched the tortilla chips and salsa right in front of us. Because she had the strength to abstain, I couldn't bring myself to eat them either, so I didn't. The funny part was she never mentioned it. We were catching up and talking about our lives, and it was such a sweet time.

I couldn't stop thinking about her. I kept replaying that lunch in my mind, reflecting on her social media posts and how much hope they gave me. Maybe, just maybe, I could do what she had done. I was nearly 50 years old. I already had one grandbaby and another on the way. Deep down, I knew this was my time. I genuinely wanted to get healthier, and I felt an urgency in my heart that now was the best and most critical time to act.

I reached out to her again and decided to go for it. I had never heard of the program before, but she boosted my confidence, making me believe I could do it and that it would work for me. We all need a little coaching sometimes. Honestly, I didn't know if it would work for me or if I could afford it, but I was determined. I sat down with Gerard, looked at our budget, and together we decided to say yes. He wanted me to feel better about myself.

A Complete God Thing

We were also thinking of finding another place to call home. We had lived in our house for 14 years, which is the longest we had ever been at one address since we got married. With my mother-in-law living with us, a two-story home was no longer practical. We needed a single-story home. We prayed, and God made a way. We found a fantastic house right in town, and it even included a mother-in-law suite. A complete God thing. He is always ready to bless His kids.

My first day was November 27, 2020—the day after Thanksgiving. I was fighting a cold or something similar, so I didn't feel my best, but I was determined to start anyway. My coach was out of the country at that time, yet she still made herself available to me. She encouraged me, guided me on what to do, and showed me how to get started.

I lost eleven pounds during the first week. Yes, that's right! Eleven! It was incredible. I quickly saw how much inflammation I had been holding onto and how hooked I was on sugar. Honestly, I've struggled with sugar my whole life. But this time felt different. I had the eye of the tiger, as I like to say. I was completely focused and determined.

The brain fog lifted, and I was able to think more clearly.

Not everyone achieves significant weight loss in their first week, and I always remind people of that. I believe my results were partly because I indulged during Thanksgiving, the day before I started! However, I also followed the program precisely. Within a few weeks, I began to feel better. The brain fog lifted, and I was able to think more clearly. I had energy for the first time in a long while; I didn't need that second or third cup of coffee after lunch. I was so excited to feel good, and staying on track was surprisingly easy. I was busy and didn't have time for meal prep. The convenience of the program was perfect!

Meanwhile, life was hectic. We were packing up our house to move during the holiday season, between Thanksgiving and Christmas. Everyone was still healing from the pandemic, and stress was everywhere. But I decided: I wasn't going to let stress stop me from this journey, and I'm so glad I stuck with it because I had no idea what was coming next.

By 2021, I was finally close to completing my college degree, and we had moved into our new home. It was my last semester, and I was excited to be so near graduation. I started back in 2015, and now, six years later, I was about to finish. Sadly, due to COVID, there was no in-person ceremony. Still, I was proud. I had worked full-time, supported my husband in ministry, and juggled all the other responsibilities that come with life, yet I kept going. Most importantly, I had finished what I started, even through some of the toughest seasons of my life.

But God's grace was always enough.

Honestly, school was an outlet for me during some of the most stressful times. I loved learning, and my classes gave me a way to keep growing even when life was heavy. Starting a church during that period was no easy task. But God's grace was always enough. He sustained us and surrounded us with support. Our pastors in Florida and our new support pastors in Alabama poured into us, shared wisdom, and helped us navigate such uncertain times. I'll never forget how blessed we felt to have their encouragement during the pandemic and as we launched our church.

Whatever you're doing, whatever goals you're setting, and wherever your journey takes you, always seek God first and good mentors second. He will never fail you, and godly mentors will help you navigate the waters when they unexpectedly rise and get out of control. God wants us to trust Him and build our community. You can do it too.

A New Coaching Venture

At the end of January, we celebrated 31 years of marriage in Mexico. It was a wonderful blessing—a time to relax, recharge, and be thankful for everything God guided us through. While we were there, I began thinking about becoming a coach with the Optavia program. It wasn't because I thought, "Oh, I need one more thing to do." Not at all. It was because I truly love helping people, and I wanted others to experience the same positive feelings I was finally enjoying.

I talked with my coach and Gerard. He was fully supportive. He was so excited about my journey and glad that I was feeling better and more confident overall. He understood how much I enjoyed encouraging others and saw the potential to make some extra income.

Looking back, it was one of the best decisions I've ever made.

In February 2021, I decided to take a leap and order my coaching kit. Once again, I had no idea what was coming. God was about to do great things in me and through me, starting with that one decision. It all began with choosing to get healthy a few months earlier. Looking back, it was one of the best decisions I've ever made—for myself and my family. Maybe for you too.

In April 2021, I had just come back from the gym and remember feeling extremely happy. What used to feel like a heavy burden no longer weighed me down, literally. I wasn't carrying that extra weight anymore, and exercising had become much easier. I was excited! I loved being able to move my body in the gym without all the pain and soreness I used to have.

My heart was overflowing with gratitude.

My new health coaching business was also gaining momentum. I genuinely loved helping people in this new way, guiding them toward better health, cheering them on, and celebrating their wins. Like life coaching, having someone in your corner who believed in you as you embraced a healthier lifestyle was a true game-changer. It was fulfilling in every way, and I could see God's blessing written all over it. My heart was overflowing with gratitude.

Life's Next Curveball

I quickly jumped into the shower to get ready for the day when I noticed a small lump. It caught me completely off guard because I hadn't seen it before. My first thought was, "Where did this come from?" I checked again. This wasn't normal. It shouldn't be there.

I had been on my health journey for about 4½ months and tracking my measurements. I had already lost nearly eight inches around my chest. I wasn't at my goal weight, but I was getting closer every day. I was building healthy habits, learning how to eat for life, and my body was changing. I felt better than I had in years. So, my mind immediately wondered, what is this? Why now?

I called my husband immediately and asked him to pray with me, but deep down I knew I needed to get it checked out. I scheduled the earliest appointment available. Meanwhile, we kept praying and reached out to family for prayer.

Here's the exact message I sent to my kids:

> "Good morning :) I just wanted to ask y'all to agree with us in prayer. Last week, I noticed a lump. I am going for a diagnostic mammogram next Monday. Daddy and I have prayed and believe it's nothing serious. I'm not concerned, but I'm trusting God. He is faithful, and He is my Healer. Thank you for agreeing with us. God's got this! I love you all."

The day finally came for my mammogram, but the images showed nothing. The technician could easily tell something was there just by looking at me, but the pictures didn't show it. So, they sent me across the hall for an ultrasound. That's when they could finally see the lump, or at least something. They explained it could be cancer, or it might not be, but the only way to know for sure was with a biopsy. I would need to come back the next week.

Now, I'm not a fan of needles, especially large ones. I'd never had a biopsy before, and honestly, I was worried I might pass out. It might sound a little funny, but I just don't handle blood or other medical stuff like bones out of place very well. My stomach flips, and I get lightheaded. A couple of times, as the kids were growing up and they would get hurt or have an accident, I was strong for a few minutes, and then Gerard would have to take over. It has become quite the joke in our house.

Let's say I am not called to the medical field!
But I'm sure thankful to God for those who are!

On April 29, I went in for a biopsy. To my surprise, I handled the entire procedure well. But when it was over, the nurse said, "Now we need to get another mammogram." What? I wasn't prepared for that. I had prepared myself for the biopsy, but the thought of doing more right away caught me off guard. My body reacted quickly; I started feeling sick, and just before I fainted, the nurse caught me. By God's grace, I was able to sit down, catch my breath, and then go through with the mammogram with a fan blowing in my face. It's a bit comical now, but it wasn't at the time. I don't think I'm high maintenance, but when it comes to these things, I am somewhat of a wimp. Let's say I am not called to the medical field! But I'm surely thankful to God for those who are!

It was a difficult experience, but I made it through. Now, all that's left is to wait for the results, which will come in a few days.

During this waiting period, I was preparing for graduation, and my parents were coming to town to celebrate with me. I had finally completed this incredible educational journey after getting pregnant in high school, eloping, and raising three young children. School had been delayed for years, and I was completely fine with that. Going back to school while working full-time and then finishing my degree felt amazing.

Still, I knew God had me

I was so excited, but at the same time, I faced all the uncertainty of this new possibility of cancer. Still, I knew God had me. I didn't know how it was all going to work out, but I had peace in trusting Him. Looking back, the timing of everything was truly divine. There's never a good time to have cancer. But when I think about making the decision to get healthy, losing those inches, noticing the lump when I did, having the mammogram and the biopsy, all of it was perfectly timed.

God is with you too. Seek Him and trust Him. Call on Him and let His warm love and grace bring you comfort and peace. There's nothing you can go through that He won't be right there with you, giving you the strength you need. He loves you that much.

May 5th arrived, and that was the day I received the call. They asked me to come into the doctor's office. At the time, I was heading to a hair appointment (and if you're a woman, you know that's a big deal because I schedule them well in advance). I told them, "You can just tell me over the phone." In my mind, I already knew what they were going to say. But of course, they don't deliver that kind of news over the phone, and that's probably for the best.

Hearing the "C-word" was shocking, even though I thought I was prepared.

I went to the office. The nurse was very kind, but she struggled to find her words. Finally, she said, "You have very early-stage breast cancer." Hearing the "C-word" was shocking, even though I thought I was prepared. She quickly reassured me that they had already scheduled an appointment with the breast cancer specialist in town. She told me this doctor was fantastic, and somehow, they had even managed to get me in the same day, within the hour. That was nothing short of miraculous, given her renowned, busy schedule and excellent medical skills.

I remember walking out and Gerard looking at me. "Are you okay?" he asked. "Yep," I said, "I'm going to be okay. Everything's going to be okay." And he nodded. "Yes, it is."

"His Name is above disease; His name is above cancer..."

We drove separately to the doctor and were now heading to another appointment. The song "Way Maker" played on the radio, particularly the part that says, "His Name is above disease, His name is above cancer..." I had never thought those words applied to me, but there I was, living it. Still, in that moment, I felt peace. Something rose inside me; it was a holy anger. I thought, "Oh no, devil, you're not going to win this fight."

God Gets All the Glory

Right there in my car, I made up my mind. I decided to worship God through this, and the devil wouldn't steal my praise or the chance to glorify God. So, I started singing at the top of my lungs: "Way Maker, miracle worker, promise keeper, light in the darkness, my God, that is who You are. Even when I don't see it, You're working. Even if I don't feel it, You're working."

It was God, right there in the car with me.

That song became a source of strength for me. It was the very first song I heard after being told I had cancer, and it couldn't have been more perfect. It was God right there in the car with me, reminding me that I wasn't walking into that next doctor's appointment alone.

We walked in and immediately saw a familiar face; someone we've known for many years. She was also a believer, and she greeted us with the sweetest smile. I can't describe how blessed I felt in that moment. Looking back, I see so much favor throughout my journey. God placed the best doctors in my path, precisely who I needed.

Jesus will be right there with us in that room.

My breast cancer doctor was nurturing, calm, and a believer. Even something as simple as the picture hanging in her bathroom gave me peace. It showed a patient lying on the operating table while Jesus stood beside the surgeon, guiding the operation. When I came out, I told her, "I like your picture. That's what it will be like for me. Jesus will be right there with us in that room." She smiled and agreed wholeheartedly.

She was the kindest doctor—full of compassion, patient with all our questions, and genuinely caring. She ordered a genetic test and an MRI so we could learn more about this tiny tumor that had suddenly appeared and was now causing so much change in my life.

Cancer was not a death sentence.
It was just a cruel disease, and it wasn't going to take me out.

When we got home from the doctor, I told my parents. They were shocked and had been praying for a different outcome, but I reassured them it would be okay. I knew God would heal me from cancer. Cancer was not a death sentence. Going to hell would be a death sentence. Hearing the Lord say to you, "Depart from me, I never knew you," would be a death sentence. Cancer was not a death sentence. It was just a cruel disease, and it wasn't going to take me out.

Ask Him and Then Offer Prayers of Thanks

That same night, I went on Etsy and ordered a shirt that said,

"Cancer Free!" I knew what I was believing for, and I also knew what the Bible says about calling those things that are not as though they were. That is what faith is all about.

For years, we exercised that kind of faith—believing and speaking before the answer arrived. This diagnosis was no different. I wasn't going to wait for a doctor to tell me I was cancer-free because I knew Jesus had already paid for my healing more than 2,000 years ago on the cross. I would just do what I always do: believe and speak what God said.

The genetic test results were positive. I didn't carry the cancer gene, which was such uplifting news! Then came MRI day, and that was a completely different experience. Have you ever been in a tight spot, unable to move a muscle, and suddenly everything starts itching? That's an MRI. You must stay perfectly still while it sounds like a never-ending alarm is going off all around you. It wasn't a pleasant experience, but God was with me even then, and I prayed the whole time. If you move, the test must restart, so I focused on staying calm, kept breathing, prayed, and remained as still as possible until it was over.

My lumpectomy was scheduled, and it looked like I would have 6-8 weeks of radiation afterward, five days a week—rigorous treatment, but worth it to eliminate this terrible disease. We were surrounded by prayer, and I was trusting in God.

Chapter 12: Cancer Free

And sing, sing your hearts out to God! Let every detail in your lives—words, actions, whatever—be done in the name of the Master, Jesus, thanking God the Father every step of the way.
Colossians 3:17 MSG

Life can be so short sometimes. We never know what each day will bring. But with God, you don't have to worry about what is next; He is there with you. His love never fails.

Just a few days after we received the diagnosis, I graduated from college. It was such a blessing to have my parents there during that time. My dad was so proud of me for my health journey and wanted to know everything I was doing. He wanted to get healthier, too, so I encouraged him to start by drinking more water. Of course, he made funny jokes about living in the bathroom, but he started drinking more, and I was proud of his efforts.

Not long after they left, I found his handwritten prayer list.

He was very impressed with the library we set up in our new home. I have always loved reading, even though, as a child, I struggled with comprehension, which discouraged me at the time. As I've grown older, I've learned to appreciate the value of reading and how much joy and peace it has brought into my life. I knew my dad would love this room in our house. I had a nice couch there, and during his visit, he spent hours reading and thinking. Not long after they left, I found his handwritten prayer list. I keep it in my desk drawer today. He retired from ministry in 2019, so now he had more time to read books, travel with my mom, and relax—a luxury he didn't always have before.

I didn't realize it, but this would be my dad's last trip to Texas and my home. I sure didn't see cancer coming in my future, but God knew. He didn't cause it or plan it, because He only has good plans for you and for me, too. Still, He can turn anything around for our good, and that is what He was about to do.

My parents gave me a strong foundation in God, which has given me solid trust in His Word.

They stayed through my graduation and the party my family threw for me. It was so wonderful to have them with me. I feel like, as a grown adult, I stand taller when my parents are around. I think, as you get older, you realize you're not everyone's favorite person. Haha! Hopefully, you will always be your parents' favorite. And you can always remember that you are God's favorite, too. Their love and support never get old, even though we do. My parents gave me a strong foundation in God, which has given me solid trust in His Word. I'm thankful.

The other day, while cleaning the guest bathroom, I saw a bottle of dog shampoo. It brought back memories of my parents' last visit. My husband had planned to give our dog, Max, a bath one evening while they were here, and he was asking where the shampoo was because it wasn't under the sink where he had left it. It turned out that my dad had been searching for shampoo one day and saw it. He had been using it every day since they arrived, not realizing it was dog shampoo. We laughed so hard, and with his quick wit, he said, "Well, it's a wonder I hadn't started barking." My dad was hilarious, and he didn't have to try very hard. He just was, and we loved every minute of it!

The pathology report came back, showing that my tumor was bigger than earlier tests suggested.

The day of my lumpectomy arrived, and everything went

smoothly. The pathology report revealed that my tumor was larger than previous tests had indicated. This raised concerns for my doctor about what might happen next. She presented my case to the tumor board. Yes, that's right! There is a tumor board where doctors gather to review cases. My situation was somewhat unique because the tumor was both noninvasive and invasive, and it was grade two, meaning it was growing at a moderate rate—not the fastest or slowest.

She also shared that my lymph nodes showed no signs of cancer, which was a relief. She explained that I had two options: one was radiation, as we had planned, and the other was a double mastectomy with reconstruction. This was a new consideration since we had initially thought I would undergo radiation. I wasn't opposed to it; it was just another option to think about.

Her reasoning for recommending the double mastectomy was that no image showed the severity or actual size of the tumor they removed. She said I was young, strong, and healthy, and found it so interesting that it appeared so quickly and never showed up on my mammogram. My doctor didn't want me to delay future diagnosis, just in case something showed up later, and the images again didn't serve me well. By removing the tumor, she said I had a 95-98% chance that cancer would never return.

We prayed about it, and God gave me peace to move forward

with the double mastectomy. It was a significant decision, but I knew it was the right choice for me. I trusted my doctor, and after meeting with the reconstructive surgeon, I felt confident this was the right path. I continued to believe, walk this out by faith, and trust God to be with me every step of the way.

The Number Eight

On June 21, 2021, I learned I was not a suitable candidate for chemotherapy. It's truly remarkable how much information can be determined from a tumor and the tests it undergoes. We sat in the doctor's office, and she explained that I needed to reach a certain number or higher to be considered a "good candidate" for chemo. I asked her what my number was, and it was significantly lower than the requirement for chemo. The best part was that it was the number 8.

"This is your healing."

I started to cry when I heard that number. Not only does it symbolize new beginnings, which are very meaningful in their own right, but the number eight also always reminds me of our eighth anniversary and the surprise wedding my husband planned. It was the day my daddy walked me down the aisle, and the day the Lord spoke into my spirit as we embraced, "This is your healing." With this special number eight marking this unexpected new season of my life, God was still speaking to me. He was right there amid it all. He continued to say, "I love you; I've got you; I will always be with you...because My love never fails. I am Your Healer."

God knows everything you are going through, every obstacle you are facing, and every mountain you must climb. He is saying the same thing to you: "I love you; I've got you; I will always be with you… because My love never fails. I am Your Healer." Listen deep within your spirit—can you hear Him? He's telling you, "This is your healing."

Still, our prayers are the most important gift we can give to those we love.

Everything was scheduled for my surgery on July 13, 2021. My dad was very worried about me and hated that I had to go through it. I told him many times that it would be okay, God had me, and I knew I was healed. My mom later told me that during every meal that season, he would pray for me. His care and concern went beyond the people at his church; they were for us, his family. When I hurt, he hurt too. I know that's how it is with your kids. I hate to see my kids or grandkids hurt as well. I want to take their place, but often that's impossible. Still, our prayers are the most important gift we can give to those we love.

The day of surgery arrived, and everything went exactly as

planned and prayed for. The Sunday before, our church family all gathered at the altar to pray for me. I felt so blessed by their faith, love, prayers, and support during this difficult time. I knew we weren't alone; we had an army of people standing in agreement with us for my complete healing from cancer. After I woke up and was transferred to my room for the night, I FaceTimed with my dad. He was so blessed to see me, and tears welled in his eyes as I told him it couldn't have gone any better. He was glad to see me and hear how well I was doing.

"You are cancer-free!"

The next day, I was discharged to go home and began my recovery. A week later, I had my doctor's appointment, and she walked in with a big smile and said, "You are cancer-free!" My husband and I were overjoyed to hear the good news and confirm what I had believed since the first diagnosis! I still had a journey of recovery ahead, but there was a bright light shining at the end of the tunnel on the road ahead!

Simple tasks that we often take for granted can become difficult. I couldn't brush my teeth or my hair properly. Taking a shower, getting dressed, and getting in and out of bed felt like chores. We don't realize all the simple movements we make with our bodies every day, but when you go through surgery, an accident, or something similar, you quickly realize how blessed we are to be able to move and do things for ourselves. I gained a new perspective and compassion for people who are bedridden, deal with sickness and disease, and don't feel their best. I don't know why so many go through these things, but I do know we're not in heaven yet. Heaven is perfect! The Bible tells us there is no crying, no dying, no sickness, no sorrow in heaven! What a place, and I pray you will be there someday too! You don't want to miss it!

He is the Overcomer

Jesus reminded us in John 16:33 (NIV), "I have told you these things, so that in me you may have peace. In this world, you will have trouble. But take heart! I have overcome the world." Also, in Isaiah 43:2 (NIV), it says, "When you pass through the waters, I will be with you; and when you pass through the rivers, they will not sweep over you. When you walk through the fire, you will not be burned; the flames will not set you ablaze." These are promises in the Word of God to us. We can know without any doubt that when we go through trials and trouble, we are not alone, and God is with us.

As I took time to rest and recover from surgery, I was able to dedicate moments to the Lord. Resting doesn't come naturally to this Momma at all. I am always on the go, like most moms. There seems to be more to do than time to do it, so this time of doing nothing while my body healed felt unfamiliar to me. I had always done everything for everyone else, but now I was in the receiving seat, and it felt strange. I was very grateful for it and for all the people who helped fill in the gaps during my healing.

I started feeling much better as the weeks went by. Unfortunately, the world began to go a little crazy again because of COVID. My parents went to an event they usually attended every couple of years and were having such a great time when, a few days later, they started feeling unwell. Of course, we didn't know what it was, but as the days went on and they felt worse, they called the doctor. It turned out they both had COVID.

It was a powerful and inspiring time of intimate prayer for the body of Christ and the world around us.

During this period, our church engaged in a 21-day prayer challenge. Over 40 people gathered each morning at 6 AM to pray. It was a powerful and inspiring time of intimate prayer for the body of Christ and the world around us. We prayed for many who were sick with COVID and for the church. These were strange times, and it seemed like just as the pandemic was ending, it was reigniting again. Everyone was searching for answers, but few were finding them. It was a frustrating and confusing time, so prayer was crucial for us all to navigate with peace and to bring comfort to those suffering.

I spoke with my parents almost every day during this period to check on them since they live in Florida, and I was in Texas. I was trying to encourage my dad, but he was very sick and wasn't himself. He was usually so joyful and positive, but he felt so terrible that it made him feel like he was dying. We didn't realize it at the time, but apparently, he was. I encouraged him one day to take communion for himself and mom to try to get his mind off the pain he was experiencing from this ugly virus. I felt terrible for them to be dealing with this awful sickness at their age. My sisters were there helping as they could with doctors and medicine, but it was such a confusing time.

My dad's oxygen level was low; he wasn't sleeping, had a fever, cough, and congestion, and felt horrible, so they took him to triage. They ran tests and worked to improve his oxygen levels. He tested positive for COVID and had pneumonia in his lungs, so they transferred him to the hospital. My mom was starting to feel better but was still very weak, so she stayed home to rest. After talking to my dad, he seemed more at ease.

My parents are both quite healthy for their age, so the COVID-19 pandemic caught them off guard. They were as sick as they have ever been before. After a day or so, Dad seemed to be improving with the medication and some rest he was getting. The next day, I was able to FaceTime him, and that seemed to help, but I could tell he didn't feel well, and he really wanted to go home.

They were calling the family now.

After a few more days, he wasn't improving, and the medicine they were giving him didn't seem to work, so they wanted to induce a coma and place him in the ICU. My mom was shocked by this news, as you can imagine. My dad rarely got sick, not even a cold, and for him to go from feeling fine just a week before to being so ill in the hospital a week later was devastating. The doctors weren't giving her much hope. Later that day, on Monday, I received a call from my brother-in-law saying they had done a chest X-ray, and his lungs were filling with fluid; his condition was worsening. They were calling the family now.

But God saw this day.

I booked a flight to arrive later that night. I had just reached the six-week mark from my surgery, and if it had been any earlier, it would have been difficult or nearly impossible for me to go. But God saw this day. He saw cancer before I did. He knew the timing, which required precision for everything leading up to that day.

I boarded that flight and prayed the entire time, hoping my dad and mom would be healed, feel better, and beat this COVID! My dad's heart rate hit 200. He kept trying to remove the contraption on his head because it was so uncomfortable, and he just wanted to go home. There were many moving parts, and it was very frustrating to understand what was happening and what was being done to help him recover. Uncertainty was obvious on everyone's faces during this time. I will never forget the devastation many families faced because of this dreadful virus.

I had been listening to a song by CeCe Winans called "Believe for It" for months, and now I was singing it over my dad.

I arrived very late, and our pastors from Florida kindly welcomed me to stay with them in Ocala, where my dad was in the hospital. Because of COVID-19 restrictions, they were tightening eligibility for hospital visits. The next day, I went to the hospital, dressed and masked, and found Dad lying in an ICU bed. I had been listening to a song by CeCe Winans called "Believe for It" for months, and now I was singing it over my dad.

I came in, and he was so surprised to see me. I told him we were all praying for him. I just sat with him, held his hand, watched his numbers, told him how much I loved him, and listened as he cried out to the Lord for help. In fact, I recorded his voice. I had never seen my dad so sick and suffering in my life. My mom and sisters came to see him that day as well. My mom was doing better, but was still very weak.

As I told him I loved him, he told me he loved me and that I was beautiful.

The next day was August 25, marking my parents' 60th wedding anniversary. It wasn't exactly how they had planned to celebrate this special occasion, but at least they were together for a little while. I snapped a picture of them holding hands in the hospital. My dad seemed stable then, and his heart, kidneys, lungs, and numbers appeared to be slightly improving. I was praying with him and talking to him, and he was coherent. As I told him I loved him, he told me he loved me and that I was beautiful. I was reminding him that he had the victory, that God was healing his body, and that he was strong. He thanked me for giving him hope, and I was blessed to capture the whole thing on my phone.

That was the day I got a marker from the nurse and wrote scriptures and encouragement on his glass windows. I also wrote thank-yous to everyone who was taking care of him. If my daddy opened his eyes, I wanted him to see words of healing and encouragement all around him in that hospital room.

Then came Thursday. He wasn't any better, but he wasn't much worse either. He was more agitated and wanted to get up and leave, but he didn't fully realize how sick he was. He was still coherent and talking to the nurse. I tried to calm him, prayed over him, and sat with him. He wanted to see Mom, and I assured him she would be there. But by the time she arrived, the doctor was waiting to speak to her, and he had no good news.

Things kept changing every hour. They began enforcing a "no visitors" policy for everyone, even in the ICU, unless it was a matter of life or death. We received mixed signals from the doctors and nurses. At first, the X-rays suggested he was improving, but then we heard reports of no change. We were all very frustrated and eager for clear answers, but they didn't seem to be coming.

As we headed back to the lobby to go home for the night, my mom sat at their beautiful black grand piano. She started playing "How Great Thou Art" and "Great is Thy Faithfulness." Worship is her default, and Jesus is whom she worships. With her mask on, she played beautiful melodies, and no one told her she couldn't. They weren't restricting her song, but they never could. Without a word, she spoke with power and grace of her faith in God. I'm so thankful I was there to witness this. She taught me so much in that moment. I will always treasure that special time in the hospital lobby.

I didn't know how, but I knew I had to keep my word to him.

Then there was Friday, August 27. I called the hospital, just as I had every morning since I arrived in Florida. This time, I was told they were not allowing any visitors. I asked for his latest X-rays so we could get a second opinion. They wanted my mom to sign a DNR and put him into hospice care, but my mom wasn't ready for that. I was prepared to go to the hospital and find out what was going on and why we were receiving such conflicting signals from the doctors and nurses. I told Dad the day before that I would come back to see him. I didn't know how, but I knew I had to keep my word to him. My family prayed for me. I was going to advocate for my dad.

After about an hour of waiting for updates on his condition, there was no real change. They planned to do another X-ray and needed to give him heart rate medication again because his heart was racing. He was becoming more anxious, wearing mittens so he couldn't remove the IVs or the BiPap machine. I knew his anxiety stemmed from not wanting to be there alone. They told me no visitors were allowed. I was aware of that, but something inside wouldn't let me leave.

The Lord kept pressing me to try again and see him.

I went to the medical records office on another floor of the hospital to ask that his latest X-rays and records be sent to his pulmonologist. After hours of waiting, playing phone tag, and getting nowhere, I felt defeated. I was no closer to them than when I arrived that morning. My heart was racing with frustration, and I started crying. I sat in the lobby in tears, thinking I couldn't leave the hospital without seeing Daddy. The Lord kept pressing me to try again and see him. So, I called the nurses' stations again and pleaded with them, but they reiterated the no-visitor policy. Still, I couldn't leave.

I went up to the ICU floor, talked to the receptionist, and heard the same story: "I'm sorry, no visitors in ICU, everyone has COVID." I asked her to give my daddy a note that said, "Keep fighting, God's got you!"

As I walked down the hall toward the elevators, I was prompted again not to leave. I had been there every day, and I knew Dad would be wondering where I was. I thought, "OK, Lord, what do I do?" He told me I needed to see him; he needed to see me, too, and he needed my prayers. I said, "OK!" So, I kept calling and begging them to let me see him for just five minutes.

Daddy, I'm here, I love you, and I'm praying for you.

After more than an hour, they told me I could stand outside his door. I stood there and called out to him. I said, "Daddy, I'm here, I love you, and I'm praying for you. Everyone is praying for you." When he heard my voice, he turned toward me. Then I did what I had seen my dad do so many times. I started praying out loud. I prayed not just for him but for everyone on the floor—the doctors, the nurses—and after about two minutes, his nurse came out of his room and said, "I'll just get you a gown."

The old saying, "the squeaky wheel gets the grease," took on a whole new meaning for me that day. I walked in and told Daddy how miraculous it was that I could visit him. I explained they weren't allowing visitors anymore, but I had the favor of God on me, just as he had taught me. I told him I loved him, and he was coherent and responded. I prayed with him, encouraged him, and reminded him that he wasn't alone because God was with him. He kept waving one hand, even though both had mittens on. He wanted to take them off, so I removed one. Immediately, he took hold of my hand. I said, "Oh, you just wanted to hold my hands," and he nodded yes. Another example of my Daddy filling that space: loving me up close. It's who he was and what he did, and he did it so very well.

I didn't realize that would be the last day he was coherent and able to communicate with me. But God did. I understand now why the Lord kept urging me not to leave and to keep fighting to see him, no matter what they said. Usually, I am a rule follower and a people pleaser, but that day I was on a mission, and I had to see it through.

She sang a beautiful song about Jesus to him.

After a few days, visitors were only allowed if they declared the patient to be at the "end of life." Dad was placed on a ventilator to support his heart rate and oxygen levels, which did improve, but nothing else was changing or getting better. Then, they called us all in to say our goodbyes because his organs were shutting down. My mom wore her pearls for the last time to see her sweetheart. She sang a beautiful song about Jesus to him. Her voice was a little shaky and weak; it was a surreal moment. I will always treasure it.

The next day, August 31, Mom decided to disconnect all the machines from Daddy because they were the only things keeping him alive. I was on my way to the hospital to say goodbye to him one last time. I planned to stay there holding his hand until he took his final breath. Once they removed everything, about two hours later, he took his last breath.

My Florida pastor reminded me that it was like my Daddy, and I experienced a full-circle moment. Being there for his last week on earth and speaking life over him was all part of our healing process. I have always been a daddy's girl, but when I got pregnant, it caused turmoil in our relationship. Over the years, God has been restoring it and making all things new. God always knew I would be with him during that last week, despite all the crazy COVID stuff around the world. He turned what the devil meant for evil into good. God is so good, and His love never fails.

We are not promised a life without end. Not me, not you. But in Jesus, there is no death; there is only life beyond life. The day will come for each of us when we leave this world. For those who know Jesus as their Savior, life becomes so much better than you can possibly imagine—no pain, no sadness, no suffering, no sickness. Only His love and grace, full of power, for eternity.

I pray you have a saving relationship with Jesus Christ. When your day comes, you will hear Him tell you what He told my daddy that day, "This is your healing."

Chapter 13: Overcoming in Him

I have told you all this so that you may have peace in me. Here on earth you will have many trials and sorrows. But take heart, because I have overcome the world."

John 16:33 NLT

Throughout all the seasons of my life, I notice a common thread. The foundation of faith planted in me as a little girl was eternal and steadfast. Even though the enemy tried many times to discourage me from believing that God was finished with me and that I was never good enough, I once even thought about ending my life. However, God was always there, showing me His love. He proved that His love is real, tangible, and able to cover me in every situation.

Love Overcomes Fear

I remember many years ago, during my time with God, one morning when I was reflecting on how much God had done for me. My heart was full of gratitude for all He had helped us through. My spirit was rejoicing as happy tears rolled down my cheeks. Then suddenly, it was like an electric thought, a revelation, or whatever you call it. I know it was from God! I realized sitting there that I wasn't afraid anymore. God had completely set me free from the debilitating fear I had lived with for so long.

It wasn't because someone specifically prayed for me at that moment or even during that season. Although I'm sure specific prayers played a part, it was simply the result of spending time with Him day after day. Keeping my thoughts focused on Him—searching for Him at the grocery store, while cooking dinner, or during a walk outside—I became more aware of His presence in my life. I know only God can do that kind of work in a person's heart. It's real, though. I pray you will experience that too. In fact, that's why I am writing this book. Ultimately, I want you to know my Friend. And He wants to know you.

Now, as we continue in full-time ministry, the enemy has opposed the vision that God placed in our hearts. We aim to help people know Christ and understand how much He loves them. We want them to have hope and realize that no matter what mistakes they've made, there is always hope, and God will never leave them nor forsake them.

Here is what he told me

Several years ago, shortly after we started our church, my dad and I were walking along the beach. I was asking him some questions about ministry, and that day I wondered what he had learned during his 45 years of ministry. Here is what he told me:

How to hear from God. (He said he was still fine-tuning this.)

How to consider his wife and treat her as a man of God should. (He said in his earlier days, he spent too much time away from his family and did not help my mom more when we were all younger. He regretted that and said he would've balanced ministry better.)

How to interact with people who have different personalities. (He told me he has always struggled with rejection, but God has really helped him to handle conflict and rejection over the years, even though it wasn't easy.)

During my battle with cancer and recovery from the double mastectomy, there were days I stayed in my pajamas and rested in bed. This was very hard for me because I am usually always on the move. Can you relate to this? I had some good days, followed by days filled with random pain. Staying still was the last thing I wanted to do, but it was the one thing I needed to do. Sometimes, I felt like

this season would never end, even though I knew it would; during the struggle, though, it was hard to see. But God was right there, carrying me through everything. He reminded me of something our pastor in Florida always said: "This is just a season, it's not your life."

It's easy to get caught up in our current situation and forget that it's just a small part of the bigger picture of life. We often see a year, or even ten years, as a long time, and usually they are. But when you consider how long life generally lasts, it's not that long.

During my health journey, I thought about the foods I couldn't eat and how much I missed them (and still do sometimes), but I had enjoyed those foods for over 40 years; that's what led me to where I am today. I guess that's why it was so hard to stop eating them, or at least avoid them most of the time, because they had become an essential part of my daily life. I was a sugar addict and loved all the junk foods—chips, Cheez-its, ice cream, candy, and sweets. But none of that helped me and only brought me closer to a prediabetic state. I never wanted to be on medication because of my weight or because I was letting myself go, so I knew I needed to change. That change led me to a much better and healthier place in life. It wasn't easy, but it was worth it. My only regret is not doing something sooner!

It's about a relationship, not a religion

Overcoming in Him isn't about living a perfect life or having everything together. It's quite the opposite. It's about when things don't go as planned, but you still know who's holding it all together for you. It's about a relationship, not a religion. As a teenager, I remember Sunday nights being dedicated to seeking the Lord at church at the altar. I would cry, pray, and talk to God about how I felt and where I was. It wasn't always pretty, but He loved me through it all. His love never fails. Human love will, but God's love never does.

I learned that victory doesn't come from trying harder, but from trusting more deeply. For years, I sought approval from those around me. This rat race left me feeling defeated. Victory isn't achieved alone; it comes through a relationship with Jesus. Without Christ, there is no victory or overcoming. All striving can end when you accept Christ into your life and all that He has provided. His sacrifice was more than enough—he literally overpaid our debt. I can't imagine where I would be without Him.

The love of God is one of the most important things you can ever experience in life. It never fails. Ever. Nothing works without it, and nothing fails with it. That is truly exciting news! The Bible tells us in Romans 5:5 (NKJV), "Now hope does not disappoint, because the love of God has been poured out in our hearts by the Holy Spirit who was given to us."

When Jesus enters your life, the Father's love is poured into your heart. This is an ongoing experience, and as you grow in your relationship, you become more aware of that love that never fails.

What will you do with that story?

When I began writing this book, I didn't know why or how I would do it. I just knew God was guiding me. I believe some of you have a story that's been building in your hearts for years. What will you do with that story? Are you ready to share it with someone? Maybe through a book, a message, a song, or a poem? I want to encourage you that it's never too late or too early to do what God has placed in your heart. If not now, when? And if not you, then who?

You'll never feel completely ready to start that business, go back to school and earn a degree, start a family, step into ministry, or write a book. You just need to take the first step. There's a good chance I wouldn't even be here to share my story if I hadn't said yes to a program that literally helped save my life that day. The timing of my getting healthy was no coincidence. God knew, and I'm so glad He led me to act instead of keep putting it off.

What are you delaying? Are you afraid to fail? Me too. Do you feel unqualified? Me too. Do you think no one will care? Me too. But what if you don't fail? What if God has already qualified you? What if someone does care? You might be the voice someone needed to hear at just the right moment. You could be the answer to someone's prayer. You could be the hope that one person is searching for. Are you willing to step out and obey what God is prompting you to do?

My prayer from the start is that my life will serve as a testament to how truly good God is and that nothing is impossible when He is your everything! He can be the peace in your chaos and the joy in your mess, and He wants to!

I challenge you to stop waiting for the perfect moment and create it yourself. God is with you, and He will help. He will send the right people at the right time. Trust Him. He's got your back. It could be the very thing that completes your healing.

I'll be right here cheering you on every step of the way! You can do it!

ABOUT THE AUTHOR

Rolanda Montenegro is a pastor, speaker, coach, wife, mother, and "Mimi" whose life's mission is to help people discover hope, healing, and purpose through God's unfailing love. As a breast cancer survivor, longtime ministry leader, and transformation coach, Rolanda provides a faith-filled perspective in every space she enters and to everyone she encourages. Her life exemplifies that God genuinely works all things together for good.

For the past ten years, Rolanda and her husband, Gerard, have led Faith Alive Church in Texas, where they lead with compassion, authenticity, and a deep reliance on the Holy Spirit. Together, they have raised three children, welcomed grandchildren they adore, and dedicated their lives to serving families, building community, and championing the next generation.

With a warm, relatable style and a message grounded in faith, grace, and perseverance, Rolanda writes to remind readers that their story matters, their voice matters, and no season is beyond God's redemption. *"Love Never Fails: The Power of Love, Legacy, and Unshakable Faith to Move You from Fear to Freedom"* is her debut book, crafted to help others find courage in their own journey and to trust the God who never lets go.

Rolanda lives in Texas with her husband, surrounded by children, grandchildren, and the church family she lovingly considers home.

Made in the USA
Coppell, TX
16 January 2026